Dedicated to so many are…

My Joe's Vet, Kate
The A team Ward A800
Consultants, Doctors Junior Doctors and radiologists
The ladies who made the worst tea and the lassie who served the best
The swinging cleaners and housekeepers
Porters that graced the corridors
The ones I never met as they put me to sleep before theatre
The team of physios who got me a bike for my birthday
My friends and family

And a young man for whom I have so much admiration, stay strong, believe and you will achieve….
Nathaniel I told you we would beat it…

Thank you all xx

In late April 2019 visiting my Vet with my little cocker spaniel Joe, Kate, the Vet noticed that my eyes and skin were very yellow and advised me to go directly and get checked out. "insisting that being a Vet she would take care of Joe but I had to see someone."

Without hesitance I attended the local hospital here in Bath, my hometown.

Into the walk in centre I trundled with my usual attitude, I'll only be here for a few mins then off to work, I never really went to the doctors but recently due to an inguinal hernia I had felt a little off colour.

My name called and the journey began, the Doctor pleasantly attended to me with the usual day to day greets and prods to the areas affected, noticing I was a little tender in and around my ribs and stomach area, also stating that I was indeed very yellow both in the eyes and across my body. He immediately called for me to attend the SUA ward and I was escorted to the ward on the first floor of the RUH here in Bath.

Taking up bed 8 in   an old Victorian ward with tall ceilings and rattly old cast-iron radiators, I was there to begin what I can honestly say has been the journey of a lifetime, in fact, if my little dog Joe hadn't had a bladder infection, through which he has fully recovered I would more than likely not started this episode of my life.

Staff immediately attending to me, name, address a bombardment of questions, including as much personal social and medical history as possible. In all my life and I must be perfectly honest its been one hell of a time, thrills, spills amongst the chaotic fast fun filled excitable and almost unimaginable 54 years. Where I had been, what I had achieved, the sports, travel and excitement, I had already totally completed most people's bucket lists and was emptying out the third or fourth to start again.

After spending an hour detailing my world to the nurse and Dr attending me, feeling humbled by the way these people doing their everyday work showed me the attention, care, compassion, faith and true respect, the treatments began. Maybe for many it would be daunting, quite frightening frankly as question yet still unanswered we're going through one's mind, but for me, well I was ill, in pain unwell, a little off colour but okay. I had an inguinal hernia that in my head maybe had twisted and caused my symptoms, how wrong was I?

The day seemed to hurry by people scurrying doing their stuff lunch and dinner served, my girlfriend Geraldine and brothers visiting, I donned my T-shirt and shorts and retired to slumber, head settling and finally able to relax I took out my phone and to my amazement my brothers had jested with one another that I resembled Homer Simpson, yellow wide eyed and somewhat strange looking, this made me chuckle as it was our way, we had always made fun of one another when opportunity rose its fruitful head.

I shared this moment with Geraldine over the phone before the goodnight and heartfelt not too worry tell kiss.

Spending the first night in my hospital bed, amongst the coughing exasperated grunts and groans of my fellow patients I was woken by a bright eyed smiley nurse at 05.30 am, being told I had various tests due today so I was, nil by mouth from 6am. Shock, horror NBM (or as my very intellectual and elder brother would say MNB) a term of endearment introduced by the

NHS to let you know you had procedures that day..

Funny really as over the coming few days you would notice the pattern of NBM patients by the sounds of crisp packets and munching continuing up until midnight and beyond.

The ward had a smell and distinctive feel about it, victorian architecture with smells of yesteryear. Nothing had changed here for over a hundred years, obviously apart from the patients and staff, my mind-space as per imagined those days with the difference of attitude and technology being the obvious..

This was to be home for the near future at least. I revelled in the attention and professionalism of all the people around me, the cleaners seemed to dance around the beds with mops gliding as if they were dancing partners, curling between beds with sweet hellos and how are you's, in accents from all over but the compassion was so uplifting, clipboards and pens caressing the items to do for the day, nurses and Consultants alike sharing information with their patients, the ward was a hive of activity but seemed to be very happy in its day..

In reflection I thought openly about my situation, I couldn't be in better hands and certainly a nicer environment, I was comfortable (apart that is from the NBM scenario) and chilled.

The consultant and his team arrived at my bedside, I was in the chair, dressed in my jeans and tee reading a book I had started many years ago and had never got to the end of.

"Good morning Simon, are you comfortable?" The usual greeting and pleasantries before he explained in detail the findings so far along with the procedures of the day. I had Jaundice, that indicated that there were underlying concerns that needed further investigation hence I would be off for a scan and X-rays today.

They left my bedside and I walked with them to the ward entrance where I acknowledged his farewell and proceeded myself to the stairs to go into the well manicured Victorian gardens to call Geraldine, after a short but to the point conversation, as Geraldine was at the Vets with Joe, I told her that I would be here for a few days pending tests and results, she agreed to come to see me after returning from our horses..

The day seemed to drag a little after this moment, mainly for the reason that no food or drink is quite painstakingly boring, especially when your up to nothing..

The large clock over the arched doorway didn't help as I could see the hands but more-so my psyche could hear the clock ticking. Be it above the rumbling of my empty tummy.

After various tests scans, x-rays and an MRI scan the team finally hit me with it. I have a mass in my stomach, a mass possibly a tumour. My whole world to change, my family along side me at the time with my great soulmate and partner Geraldine, The consultant broke the news. We looked at each-other and the air of silence seemed to stand still, it was eerie, incredible to even digest, I seemed to go numb and for the next few minutes I could see people around me nodding heads opening mouths, tears and wiping of eyes but I could feel and hear nothing, the team of consultants and nurses left us all, in that moment I knew I was going to rise and bring a smile to everyone's face. Oh! Yes I did, quipping one of the many sayings I had often expelled in times gone, "ok, here we go again, we know what we're up against and the blindfolds off, let's have this fight, and with you guys and the team here in my corner it's going to be a good fight with me coming out on top"… After visiting hours had passed everyone gone and Geraldine and I had shared a hug and kiss goodnight at the entrance to the main hospital, I was in a world where I knew everyone who knew me would stand with me and I had this incredible team of nurses, Doctors, consultants and staff stepping up to the plate, my new found friends and caring team had taken me in. With this is my head and being somewhat in disbelief I managed to get myself motivated to go for a stroll back though the long tunnel like corridors of this establishment. The one thing that was so obvious to me here was that although I was on my own I had a great feeling of being, my heart felt the warmth and whilst I wandered off I knew I was in good hands with vey special people behind me. These moments somewhat seemed to be the way of being for me here and I was able to find my bed before I realised. A welcoming bed in a place others would find stressful or even frightening, I was at peace, able to undress and put on my shorts and sleep..

Like the hare running I was up with the birds 6.30am, things to do, no sitting on my laurels, I had the bit between my teeth and was on full throttle. Only to be brought back down by the voice from the nurse "where you off Simon?" I'd been caught off guard and felt like the scared rabbit as I was told to get back as breakfasts on its way. My breakfast was good and past an hour, I know an hour for breakfast shame on me. It was good all the same, cereal, toast and tea reviving my enthusiastic spirit but also giving me the thinking time.. I revisited the words of yesterday, digested and happy I felt the need to be doing something, what? The 64k dollar question, what was on the cards for me now? In hospital we all have time, thinking is not something I like to do too much, firstly it's quite painful and secondly I'm a doer, actions speak louder than words...
A plan was needed but where do I begin? I had to think of me, as it was my life and I had to be selfish for once, always a giver never a taker me but I need this to focus my energy on me. I'm

not saying anything but just let's put my positivity into my world and build my strength up for me.. Bravado is great and helps with others who are dealing with things, a false front is only self deception, I use my sense of humour to get through certain things that others would hide from, yes, I'm scared, I'm bloody petrified and for what I'm in good hands, the best team is on my side. That's a fact, it's not difficult for me to see this but most of our lives it's us who make things complicated, our ability to blame is immensely frustrating. We make choices and should accept the responsibility of those choices, accepting sometimes is hard however I have discovered that the pathway is sometimes a little over grown and occasionally we have to wait for things to clear before we can pass, the storm maybe ahead of me but I will pass and again I can continue on my simple journey through life. Riding the waves as never before.

The dawn broke and I was awake through the large cold pane of glass I could see the trees and clouds of the sunny April morning, imagining the air and smell of the dew I took a large breath, deep into my lungs I held onto that moment, savouring it as if it were my last. Realisation had made me sleep well and I felt at peace with my new found situation, only I knew how I felt, it's true, people try to understand, say they know how you must be feeling, their compassion being somewhat misconstrued as selfishness, a true misinterpretation of what you're going through seen through their eyes... we all have the best intentions in these times we all long to say the right things but in truth I believe we should look forward, stay silent of the past and make small steps into the future. Positivity will enlighten the saddest of times, be it through silence, laughter or even the sweetest of smiles.. We all have to ability to drop our heads, curl up into a ball and ask why me? However in realism our own self belief, self preservation if you like should be totally the opposite, hold ones head high, look to the future and strike off the best foot forward in a great but simple way of getting to the light at the end of the tunnel. For this was my way, I had been in situations many times before, not really knowing the outcome, not fully understanding the reasons why, but I got through. Stubbornness maybe sometimes had

pushed me but I still had got my act together and motivated myself forward. The light at the end of tunnel occasionally dimmed but to me I just kept moving on, convincing myself that I was on a slow bend. This therefore was yet another curvy but still albeit dim lit tunnel...
The start of a new day had enlightened me into a second wind, not that I needed much drive in that sense of being. I felt the need to get on with something, I took a cold shower, invigorating my blood through my veins and returned to me bed feeling brand new and full of positivity, I pulled the curtain around me and donned my jeans and a t-shirt socks and trusty old boots, deciding that I was to go for a stroll through the hospital gardens and look on as the first of the trees began to throw new colour into our world. I loved the blossom and smell of the land it was something that Geraldine and I had created out where we kept our beautiful family of horses, our very own piece of heaven. Ready to go I pulled the curtains back tightened my belt and like the greyhound chasing the hare I was off, I got to the end of the ward and let the smiling young nurse know I was off for a little walk, in a way I didn't even give her time to

respond, with a smile and wave I was gone along the long narrow corridor through into the gardens, as I pushed the doors open I felt the coolness of the breeze hit my face and my lungs filled with the springtime air...

I walked pondering over my life and all the treasured memories I had made, I'd had a life full of excitement and fun times with good friends, strangers that many becoming friends in sharing my laughter and the fondest of times over the years. People talk of bucket lists and living the dream of life, travelling and sharing memories later in life however I had filled various buckets of all shapes and sizes with the best and worst of experiences imaginable. Breaking my stride and taking the bench by the pond under the willow I spread my arms across the back of the bench, gazed to the sky and the vastness above was savoured in that moment. My experiences had made me the character I am today, captured the world and given me the memories of a somewhat extraordinary life, some moments had made their mark for good or bad but I had made it through, the unselfishness of my attitude towards others had shown me how easy life can be, by being simple you can achieve more, the smaller steps the easier the journey. I sat, my thoughts meandered from one memory to another and time passed by so slowly it seemed, I had been there for at least an hour before my tummy, my body clock called for sustenance, yes, I was peckish, a thing that if you knew me most definitely could change or influence me, feed me now, I was like Grover from the muppets when hungry I needed something and it had to be now. Up in flash I made my way back into the grand hallway of the hospital that led me directly into the terrace restaurant, it was like my GPS had honed into the nearest food outlet, the smells were amazing, food glorious food, fresh coffee and the clinking of knives and forks, people chattering over mouthfuls of good old fashioned fodder, checking my finances I took a large tuna filled baguette, side salad with a double expresso, yummy!! My first mouthful was delightful, my engine room soon began to express its gratitude... life is good where food is involved, loving food and full flavours were a massive part of my existence both socially and romantically, it had shown me how to bring a group of people together and also the healthiness of a good regime can result in one's time shared with another leads to a great relationship, in all my relationships with my family friends and loves we had always ate good food and made great conversation over the table, sometimes the best tables were just two but more often than not it would become many more, people love to eat and chat, especially if the food and camaraderie was full of fine flavours and banter of the best.

After my late breakfast early lunch I walked aimlessly back to the ward, along the way seeing a face I recognised striding toward me, it was the consultant, in conversation with a colleague doing their rounds, I raised my eyes to attract his attention and politely excused myself in interrupting their chat, I asked if I could have a word or two, his reply was "I'll come to see you Simon I just have to speak here for a few minutes and I'll directly with you"
That few minutes seemed to trigger in me the way I had felt on numerous occasions in my days as both a rugby captain and achiever the desire to raise our game. He came to my

bedside after a somewhat longer time than imaginable and asked if I was ok,

"Yes, I'm fine and would like you to be frank with me please, how does it look? What are our plans and what can I do to aid in our dilemma?" A few questions he had not expected, I could tell by the expression and somewhat intriguing look in his eyes, his reply came as directly and honestly as my questions themselves. " it is a tumour Simon, in a very difficult place and I have called for a meeting of consultants and specialist in this field for asap, being the bank holiday weekend you can appreciate it may not be held until Tuesday, but it will be this coming week I can assure you" my reply was quick and to the point, " I'm in your hands now and knowing the team I have behind me and your team beside me I'll be the strength we all need to get the result we need"

His eyes grew through his glasses and he stood before me, as I raised from the side of the bed his words were somewhat enlightening as if he had a great confidence in my attitude, he spoke " it's the weekend Simon would you like to go home and spend time away from here, be with your family and friends and I assure you we will catch up after the holiday weekend, my team will meet and we will contact you as soon as" Words that make you smile are the best in the world, the best imaginable, I felt my smile beam and patted the man on the shoulder shook his hand and thanked him, with the biggest smile and words "you've made my day, thank you." The next few minutes were a frenzy of phoning Geraldine and asking her to come get me, letting my brothers and family know my somewhat surprisingly good news and packing up my little bag of belongings, also the nurses and sister had to prepare my papers for discharge. Their faces were so happy for me they seemed to spend the next few minutes solely on my happy news. Yes, I know it was a good thing I was soon to be at home within my world for a few days however the reality was it was decision made in true compassion, I was strong in myself, my health be it in turmoil was somewhat ok but I was more than able to get up and go, certainly able to fend for myself for the next few days. Maybe the consultant could see this in my attitude and had made his decision based on my well being and positivity, it certainly was the best way forward for me. I thanked the staff and made my way to the car parking area at the end of the wing of wards.

Greeting me with a big Cheshire Cat smile was Geraldine, I could make her out as the sliding doors opened, sun filled my heart as there they were sat in the big green Land Rover with little Joe strewn across her lap, gazing toward the entrance as I emerged. The excitement in all of us was exhilarating, a feeling of true love came over me and I ran towards the truck, launching myself at the window, arms stretched out, I was where I needed to be. We spoke for a few moments and I played with Joe in the front as his tail frantically swished to and fro in excitement of his daddy's return. The familiar sound of the defender starting up, the roaring engine never sounded this good, I was out of here, we were a tight unit once again.
We drove directly towards the town centre, not really noticing the bank holiday traffic, the people, as the defender seemed to float through the busy town streets towards the countryside where Geraldine had without even having to ask knew I wanted to be, yes we arrived at our little piece of heaven, the land

where our time was spent with the horses, lounging, playing, but most of all enjoying what we had both worked hard to keep and create, our garden of paradise. The horses had heard the Land Rover coming down the road and the distinguished sound of the chains around the gate made them all look up simultaneously towards the double gates, they struck off one by one, familiarity in their strides as they made way towards the gate. Geraldine had already been up this morning to feed and turnout the guys so their intrigue in us being back so soon had taken over from eating the lush spring grass and they wanted to know why we were here. Yorkie the herd leader strutted his stuff and was first to greet me at the gate, in his usual manner he sniffed each of my hands and nudged me with his large dew filled nose, his way of being attentive and showing you he cared, Yorkie was indeed the leader in both prowess and manner, he was a lovely bay gelding, totally in awe of himself and at times a true bugger, we loved him, many would never have stood for this but his eyes and softness at times drew you in. He was 17'2 a powerhouse of 22 years with the playfulness of a 12 year old, he was more than capable, but he would make you work for it, and by work I mean work. It was his way or no way, we knew this and Geraldine had made her mind up, Yorkie or sneaky snorkel as she lovingly called him was here and nothing would take him. Majestically he knew this and paraded through his day in the knowing. As always after his majesty, we had the rest of the herd following up behind, Howdy, Tiep-Tiep, Timmy, Chance and finally the ever present and loving Jaffy bringing up the rear, even though he was the eldest and most probably the most capable he was like a librarian, always like, after you, please after you, Jaffy, had a self preservation mode and never put himself in a situation where he felt threatened or uneasy, he was a true gent in all, both with us and the other horses. They all greeted me with the usual expressiveness, of what you doing here? Is it feed time again? I was home with all my friends and in the place we all loved. Geraldine parked up and we strolled into the fields, taking in the freshness of the spring and warm midday sun on my face, I was once more in my heaven. Spending the afternoon chatting and doing horsey stuff, well her ladyship did the work as I looked on, I said to Geraldine " go on love tack up and ride Tiep." I didn't need to repeat myself, they all were brought in and into their respective stables they wandered as if like clockwork, they had a good routine and as said before they were our friends so we stuck by them and the regime that worked. Tiep was in his stable and given a good groom before saddle and bridle were put on, he looked a picture of health did Tiep, he had come to us through a good friend, he had raced a few times but had an injury and consequently was in need of a home to reestablish himself back into maybe a different life from racing. Tiep was great doer he loved to please and enjoyed his time, always playing in the field, showing off, he was 12 going on 8 shorter than our other guys 15'3 maybe 16 hands but he was full, he had the most magnificent power and was like a Ferrari, a little naïve and somewhat unsure of what his new home expectancy was but we weren't even bothered we just loved him as was, he'd been with us a few years now and both Geraldine and I loved how he was, one of our friends had evented him, another had taken to a couple of local dressage competitions and we had both had lessons with him, Tiep suited us, good fun a little minxy at times but he could fly and give you a great moment, you know like the round of golf, you may have had the worst day ever but that couple of shots were something that seemed to make it all worthwhile. Once in the school Tiep was ready for work, Geraldine mounted and he was straight into it, they looked so good and seemed to be having a great time, as Joe and I watched on from our little seat in the corner, they popped over a couple of little jumps and played as they should, after twenty or so minutes you could tell Tiep had had enough he got bored too easily and showed it, the time was now for Geraldine to get him to work through it, make him work even harder, almost telling him off she got him going again, her confidence grew and he knew the actions he had to take before they were done.

With the guys in and Tiep ridden we topped up their nets and went off for a coffee before returning for their evening feed and rugs before bed.

This was our piece of heaven the getaway where we spent most of our time.

On returning home, as we lived in an apartment in the centre of Bath we took our time to climb the stairs and swung open the heavy Georgian door, home at last, nothing beats it, the smell of our lives, very welcoming. Joe ran to get his toy stoat and jumped straight into his bed by the kitchen door, he also had a routine, in the door, grab my toy, to my bed and watch daddy prepare my tea, his eyes following me around the kitchen, scrutinising my every move, tail wagging in anticipation of his culinary delights, chicken, broccoli carrots and rice filled his bowl, minutes passed and he was gulping down copious amounts of water to wash it all down, back to stoat and on his other bed, displaying his thanks in rolling from side to side with legs all in the air, tossing stoat too. He was a happy Joe...

We had our meal and I ran a warm bath as I was quite tired, in fact this past week had been quite a rollercoaster for all of us. I so wanted it all to be a dream as I lay in the warm water with the hot tap trickling over me, I felt myself falling into a warm sleep..

To be home, relaxing with both Joe and Geraldine gave me a great sense of love and being.

It's amazing how we as people take so much for granted, here the three of us ate, bathed, slept and maybe on the odd occasion relaxed, we had it all, it was a lovely home, a real cosy and warm environment with no television and no central heating, if we felt the cold we would either put on more clothes, light the gas effect fire in the lounge or cuddle up in bed with books or a magazine, I loved our simplicity, in winter months I had been deemed very often to be in bed before 8pm, only to have to walk Joe a bit later for his final time before 10pm as he would then join me in the warmth of the covers for a while sometimes sleeping at least until 6.30am. On others occasions he'd sleep at the foot of the bed in the curved cushioned end with his legs in the air..

Such a big part of our lives was Joe and really if when I think back to when this all began and how I'd taken Joe to the vet with his bladder issue, I'm absolutely sure that this little friend had been my saviour, the fact is I would've never attended the hospital that day.

Geraldine and I exchanged few words over the next few hours we ate a lovely supper of fish and salad, washed down with lime and ginger infused water whilst listening to the hustle and bustle of the busy street below. I washed the dishes and ran Geraldine a nice hot bath as she took Joe to the park for his evening doings. On return I was already in slumber, under the covers, feeling snug in our own lovely big cozy bed.. Nothing quite like it.

Morning sunshine and the birds woke me from a lovely deep sleep, up and at it already a pot of coffee was placed at my side and this was followed with a large glass of nutrition, an infamous smoothie consisting of fresh fruit and ginger, a new day a new kickstart. Soon up and out Geraldine had decided I was staying in bed and she would attend the horses and bring breakfast back a little later. I had time to savour the coffee and relax into the fluffed up pillows, eventually falling back into sleep only to be woken by a frantically excited scampering sound of Joe as he returned with mum from the horses, a happy little fellow strewn across the duvet, brown eyes following my every thought. "Morning darling, breakfast in bed is it? We have spinach, bacon, eggs and tomatoes on sourdough."

" yes please." This was our way, we regularly had time on a Sunday to take breakfast together and it set us up for the day ahead. We sat and spoke of the goings on that had surrounded us over the past week, Joe was on the mend after his procedure and he seemed to be well on track to a full recovery, my journey however had really only just started, we discussed the way we felt and all about what we knew, which was very little really, we knew of the tumour, where it was, and the up and coming meeting but still we felt a little blinkered in our understanding of how we would be moving forward. I had an idea that the situation obviously was being dominated by my positivity, albeit considered through others eyes as bravado. I was in the hands of the best there was. I had no reason for doubt, therefore every thought could be strength building. We met with friends, my brothers and savoured the few days we had together both with our animals and each-other, it felt surreal to me not to be thinking of work, reacting to phone calls or emails, just time for us.

The call came on Tuesday afternoon I was to attend the hospital this week on Friday at 2.15pm at the radiology dept on the ground floor. With this in mind I knew I had at least a week ahead of sorting things for us, work wasn't a priority but I had clients that had to be put in the picture, I had the hernia and was able to use this as an excuse to put off their work, it seemed strange to be prioritising and adjusting my work for I had always loved what I do but for once my health took priority over my income. Mostly the task was easy a simple email would suffice, but a couple of clients needed to be informed face to face, not that they were anything special and by that I mean treated any different they just came across as the only ones whom I relied upon for my work, the pick up the phone and expect you attend straight away types. Delicately I dealt with them, making sure they fully understood my situation without the need for them to know everything. People needed to know as much as I felt was necessary however some needed to know everything, how crazy these times are, gone are the days of trust and respect, if you put yourself out for people they saw it as a sign of weakness, the more you gave they more they'd take, "givers have limits, takers don't," rang in my ears. I'd spent so much of my working life giving my all to get the best results, sometimes over and above all I had expected but I still gave more, now it was time for me, almost as if I needed a kick to change my ways, a harsh kick, this was certainly an eye opener.

The next few days were spent with all I loved around me, we were at the horses, playing with Joe in the woods, eating and enjoying the fruits of life, Geraldine and I spoke a lot, sat in silence too, it was how we were. Our time was uncomplicated, we knew how to be happy and how to achieve a sense of freedom from the stresses and tribulations of everyday life, we had no distraction, very rare did we talk about the state of the nation or the great big world beyond. We had our life and it was easy but with hard work involved.

Friday soon came and along with my two younger brothers we attended the RUH in Bath, David and Andrew were there for support and it filled me with the strength knowing this. I was a little apprehensive of course albeit only a CT scan, it still was alien to me and somewhat scary, today was finding out more, how far had the tumour spread, how big it was, the questions yet unanswered were going to be thrown in to the frame and somehow the surgeons, consultants and team were going to piece a plan of action together, this is what today was all about, this was now my life in their hands. How scary is that? The beginning of the next chapter was to be determined by today's investigative outcome. Before in the waiting room we sat and I was told to drink cold sips of water for at least 45 minutes, quite an ask really, I felt slightly nervous and that usually made me feel like I needed to take a wee. I could feel the coldness of the chilled water against the hot flushes of my anxious body, I began to get agitated and fidgety, my brothers were aware of this and as we do in theses circumstances we began to giggle at the silliest of things, what were we laughing at? It was not normal actions of three middle aged men, more like naughty little schoolboys waiting outside the headmasters office. The time seemed to pass by and finally my name was called and we rose simultaneously before the radiologist, somewhat dwarfing her, almost by timing her authority kicked in as she said, "Simon please." Both brothers looking directly at me gave her the chance to say " thank you, wait here, we will be about twenty minutes."

I asked if one could come in with me just for reassurance and also as I knew myself in these circumstances I wouldn't really listen and was more likely to miss something, Andrew agreed to attend with me. Taken to a small area I was told of the procedure and what it entailed, pretty much all the things I was told before the first scan only this time the surroundings were less eerie, the large room was bright and airy with a lovely montage over the large doughnut shaped scanner, this gave the place a defining air of being in a conservatory, looking out to the blue skies above, the three radiologists got going and Andrew waited outside as they performed their duties in the most compassionate way. Before I knew it I was back with my brother Andrew in the small cubicle adjacent to the scanner room. The nurses came to see if I was ok and asked if I could rest there for twenty minutes just to be sure that I didn't feel any effects like nausea or giddiness.

Andrew asked the questions I wanted to ask myself, the results we were told, would be with us in seven to ten days dependant on the scan but being a Friday it would be at least a week. What did I need to do now?

"Go home and just await the call, I'm sure they'll contact you if there is anything further." She said.

The doors to the waiting area outside swung open and standing there was David with a big grin, happy to see me smiling he patted my shoulder and we marched out of the hospital back to his for a well earned coffee and chat. On the walk back I dropped behind a little so I could reassure Geraldine over the phone, she after all had been my rock through these trying times. In our life together we had had a few moments and to be frank for some reason we had made headway together, that definitely is an understatement, and truly another story for another day..

The coffee pot boiling, the aroma of which infused the air we stood chatting in the kitchen, as like all brotherly conversation it soon turned to banter maybe to some a little dark and even inappropriate but it was fun.

I'd always loved liver and onions and for some reason I felt the need to make light of my situation in such a way..

I so loved my brothers.

David dropped me back into town a bit later that afternoon.

The weekend was upon us and I wanted it to not be any different so Saturday morning we drove to the horses and took breakfast with us, Joe and I walked the fields as Geraldine mucked out the stables and fed the guys. Joe soon let me know it was his time for breakfast too and we made way back up to the lodge to have our treats, Joe had chicken and broccoli, we had fruit bread with fresh fruit and coffee, we knew how to enjoy food, sat in the early morning sun amongst the wildlife and listening to the horses eating their breakfast too, nothing beats it, everyone's a winner. Horses happy now and ready for the off, Geraldine opened each stable and the sound of hooves on the concrete alerted the birds, the guys were on route.. Gate opened and they were gone, bucking, kicking out they shot out towards the sun drenched bottom field. They played like spring lambs for about ten minutes before the sweet smell of the spring grass caught their tastebuds and as if like magic, all our horses were munching the lush green grass.

They were quite contented in their world and we were too, our incredible way of life..

That afternoon I sat in the new lodge with Joe aside me on the sofa. We dozed for a bit as Geraldine prepared the jumps in the school for her to ride a bit later. Not everyone's existence but it suited us and I loved it when it all came to plan, Geraldine loved to play up here and I obliged in helping her as best I could. We had a great life...

The weekend passed and with the week ahead we planned to visit a few friends, just be together whilst awaiting the next call. It was Monday around Twelve-thirty that my mobile rang, I was driving, my phone showed no caller ID, pulling over we looked at one another and I answered, my nervousness apparent to Geraldine as I said "good afternoon Simon here."

" good day can I speak with Simon Manister please?"

My jaw dropped as I heard the words and with an element of both fear and abruptness I said, " today, what right away?"

Geraldine's eyes were fixed on mine as I said goodbye…

"The hospital, that was the hospital, I have to go back in today love, into the hospital today."

"Ok, don't worry now, what was said, exactly what was said babe?" Geraldine's tone as per usual sending a calmness through me.

" I have to go back into there today, the BRI in Bristol ward A800 on the eighth floor, by three pm, ok?"

Already knowing that I had lost my senses a little, Geraldine told me to drive back to the flat and pick up an overnight bag and she would then drive me to the hospital this afternoon.

In fact she drove me to Davids and he drove me to the hospital in Bristol. It was a surreal journey, I already missed my family and friends but didn't understand why…

Really I don't know how I came to get to the ward even the hospital but I arrived just before the time they had asked, I hated being late even for this, I was shown to a room on the ward, Room 30, a single hospital bed with a big window and table and chairs, behind a large double door was a shower area and toilet, my own room with en-suite. Wow! How was I given this, what was it all about? I dropped my bag by the bed and within moments a nurse introduced herself and asked if I was ok?
This was it now, my time was in their hands...

I phoned Geraldine and explained how things were, she almost knew I would be ok, the thought of finally things getting done were pleasing to her. Her mother was a retired nurse with over 30 years in nursing and that had had an effect on how Geraldine approached our situation, sympathy was shown in a very abrupt manner with a get on with it attitude taking the fore. David and I sat and chatted in the room when Paul and Andrew arrived, feeling a little more like the old me I spoke with the nurse behind the desk about my situation and it seemed that I was to be seen in a few moments, when all would be explained to us in due course. Within minutes a consultant came to the door and entered introducing himself firstly to me then my three brothers, it was a very brief introduction in which he explained the way they were planning the next few days, he was to return tomorrow morning and would have a more detailed itinerary for us.. I asked if there was any reason I couldn't go out for a walk to which he replied, "not at all this is your room here and you can come and go as you please, enjoy you walk." joking and smiling we left the ward.

It seemed strange as we strolled out of the main entrance, passing the designated smoking area where patients and staff alike were getting their last gasps of smoke into their lungs before discarding the butts and re- entering the large foyer of the hospital, back to their wards, it seemed incredible really.

Pressing the button to the pedestrian crossing all four brothers crossed the road and veered left towards the small rank of shops and cafes up on the hill. Obviously we were heading into somewhere for chat and a coffee, the city was a hive of activity and people like soldier ants were busying through their days, phones in hand, ears engaged in listening and totally oblivious to others around them they scurried and skipped. We came to the top of Christmas Steps and took a left as if we were in the know of where we were going, just talking generally about nothing but we were engaged in deep thought, at the bottom we stopped and spun around to see a little somewhat intriguing shopfront with old fashioned board games and memories of our childhood, it was a gaming café but not the modern type with consoles and iPads, this was a board gamers paradise, everything from Cluedo to Ker.plunk, on entry we were approached by a flat capped young man of about 25 asking us if we were in for game night or just coffee and drinks, wow! I can tell you it brought many memories flooding back for all of us, the afternoons the rows and mostly for me the days of travelling to and from Bath to Romford to spend holidays with our cousins. We sat at a table and the chap brought over the menus, coffees smoothies and drinks galore, but on the reverse they had a food menu, it looked great and soon the desire of coffee had changed to food and smoothies… A real belly bash was underway and we ate drank and reminisced for a good few hours before heading back. We parted company at the steps and David and I headed back over the road to the ward within the hospital. David sat with me for about half hour and making sure I was ok, finally he left. I tidied my things and got into some form of comfort before calling Geraldine to let her know I was in good hands and had had a fun time with the brothers. It was now nearing 9.30pm and I was tiring fast, would I sleep well? I don't know, a strange bed one thing, even more was the environment, I wasn't used to hearing people shuffling trolleys back and forth, conversations between nurse and patient. The night stood still and finally I drifted off…

"Good morning Simon, how did you sleep?" Came the welcoming voice of the young male nurse.
He came to do my observations, blood pressure, heart rate, temperature and oxygen levels, Like a Pre Mot on your car thus determining whether you had any underlying issues before they start the day.

"All is fine Simon and you seem ok, did you manage to sleep?

Would you like a cup of tea, coffee?" He asked.

"Yes I'm ok and slept well, I'd love a tea thanks milk no sugar." Came my reply, as I noticed the clock on the adjacent wall, it was only 5.35am and already they had me engaging in the day ahead. Another more senior nurse entered and introduced herself, she proceeded to perform her duties whilst chatting away and telling me about her daughter's escapades from the weekend, it felt so easy as they just talked, done their thing and got on. Bloods were taken next and a cannula was fitted to my right arm. She was on her way. I took my time to readjust my head and gently laid back on the bed, looking through the big window I noticed the pigeons fluttering across the window ledges in the morning light, they took up their positions for the start of their day. One very distinctive thing was very noticeable from the window, it was the helipad above on the roof of the ninth floor. I'd heard the shuddering blades in the night and thought it could've been the venting on the roof but not so, it was a large landing pad for the emergency helicopters..

This place was vast absolutely amazing in comparison to the old hospital wards in the RUH. I had a room with shower a TV and radio and multi tasking compassionate people in and out all day, all showing me how this vast institution ticked so incredibly. I drifted back to sleep for about an hour only to be woken by a tap to the door, a sweet voiced lady was in the doorway and asked me if I'd like breakfast, she made tea and I had porridge followed by orange juice and a slice of toast, I never ate this much first thing, but I felt the need for food, a comforting that most people took for granted.. I loved good food and always considered it as a fuel in my days of work and play, even more so now I had the horses in my life. After breakfast I took a shower and got into my real attire, jeans and shirt, put on my boots and asking the ward nurses if I was needed for anything, I was off to familiarise myself with the vastness of this place. To my amazement there seemed to be many people already dwelling about the corridors and elevators. A real factory of well being, if you can understand my trail of thought. People visiting loved ones, porters, cleaners and nurses filing their way through the avenues from floor to floor. I viewed the seagulls taking in the sunshine across the rooftops of Bristol which seemed to stretch for miles, chimney pots and towering high raised buildings gave way to cranes and bridges in the distance, I could see as far as Westbury Wiltshire, some where that only a few weeks previously Geraldine and I had walked with Joe.. Kelston Tump and Lansdown, Toghill and the tower at Ozleworth in Gloucestershire, the skyline was incredible. I was in the heart of Bristol and this life saving place was alive with a pulsating ambience. I knew I couldn't drift far from the ward as the doctors were doing their rounds and would need to speak with me, therefore I wandered back, being greeted by good mornings and hellos that echoed the friendly feelings of the establishment. It was reassuring as I'd always imagined hospitals as places of sadness and hardship, but here it was totally the opposite, smiles and eyes met with feeling. As I walked the horseshoe shaped ward to my room a group were gathered in the hallway adjacent to the nurses station, were they here for me?

I skipped past and took to the seat near the window, soon to be back to my feet and welcoming in the team that would be part of my ongoing story, the next few minutes were inspirational, daunting and a little numbing too, I had knowledge of some of my situation but now I was to be told a much fuller picture, the accounts of all were explained in detail and yes, I had a tumour that was constricting the ducts below my liver causing me to be jaundiced and indicating that I had a very serious issue that would require various procedures that may result in me having more of my life back. They asked me about my life, family and general things but we knew why we were here, I had to know the full scenario, asking questions always gave me a better picture of the fight I had ahead and this was my way of taking on such obstacles, an old school friend had always said to me that life is for living and no matter what it throws at you, there is no storm you can't ride, "it's not the ferocity of the storm it's the way you learn to dance in the rain." I can see his face even now.

For many, I think the next 15 minutes would have seemed terrifying but it brought me enlightenment and I finally felt I was beginning to know more of the scenario we were all facing, the team were amazing, giving the confidence and exposure of facts that I required, I began to realise the simple fact that the more we all know and relate to one another the easier the journey for all would be, we were after all striving for the same outcome.Team was in place and ready to go.

Blood taken, statistics and observations done we were on our way, I had now met with the the surgeon who would be performing the first procedure, she arrived that afternoon when two of my brothers were visiting, a very quiet spoken woman, direct with her explanation of how things would commence, the procedure was called a laparoscopy, a type of surgery that allows the surgeon to access the inside of the tummy with very small tools and a camera mainly to examine the organs and identify the relevant problem areas. I felt myself drifting off and had to explain that I wasn't being rude but I had an urge to lay back and listen with my eyes closed, if I missed anything I'm sure my brothers would pick up the necessary points that I may have not mentioned, or dealt with. It's how I was, I knew myself well enough to digest the points I needed too. We all stared at one another and questions were answered, as and when, the surgeon left and we again took a moment each to reflect before speaking, "Wow! That was a revelation, so direct and to the point, how do you feel about that then guys?" Paul said with hands to the sky. "There's knowing your stuff and then there's that, absolutely amazing, it just fills one with confidence, don't you agree?" David piped up. What a team, this was literally how it had become, my life in their hands and if things were as direct and that straightforwardly explained we were in the hands of the best. It seemed to lift the mood and I couldn't wait to share it with Geraldine and friends, Paul had already stated that we should let everyone know as soon as, obviously we had a brothers forum set up via social media that was fabulous as we could all see the messages we were sending, but mum, well that would be down to me as I felt a little protective and feared mums need to know too much would cause her unnecessary concern, in fact we still didn't know exactly how far the tumour had spread and the extent of the seriousness, therefore mum didn't need to know. There also was the issue of dad, he was in a home and he'd been there for a couple of years now, he had dementia and mum had to deal with this too. Imagine being together each day in a relationship that spanned over 65 years, suddenly to have to deal with being alone at home, no one to share those nights with, waking and going to bed, eating and even cooking for one, my poor mum had all this on her mind, it was ok for my dad, Brian, he was being well attended too, had people around him 24/7 fed, watered and generally pampered over with the addition of other residence, I know dementia is hard for those with it, but even harder at times for the ones at home alone..

It seemed like all must be coming at once but my mum was a toughie, or at least she gave that impression. I still felt the need to protect her. So after my brothers and I had gone upstairs to the café for a coffee and then all took leave on the way back to the ward, I called Geraldine and explained all about the days events, I could hear an air of anxiety in her voice. I didn't feel the desire to protect her in such a way as I had my mum, Geraldine and I had been through a lot together, both sad and fun so we knew one another well enough to say it as it was, and indeed I did exactly that. The sense of relief was incredibly uplifting and I felt Geraldine's demeanour change, albeit over the phone, we carried our chat on for a few more minutes and I too had a chat with Joe, he responding with the typical wag of the tail and shaking from side to side, I could picture him so well. It was now time for tea and because I knew maybe this would be that time when nil by mouth could come, I engaged in a real feast, eating all the hospital food and some of my own delights, I had an array of goodies in my room as well as various juices and teas from all corners of the globe, ginger and turmeric with a hint of lemon, lapsang souchong, green teas and peppermint infused tea, such delights. A banquet fit for a king.

More attention followed soon after with medications and the fitting of the cannula, this was used to administer the medication required directly into the vein, it all was and felt alien to me but I was here for that reason, to do whatever it took. No pain no gain.

There was no let off for the next few moments, bloods taken, observations made I was weighed too, feeling as if I were going into a situation more like a boxing tournament than a medical procedure I felt ready. NBM was from midnight which indicated to me that the first steps would start very soon the next day, it was now fast approaching 10pm and I needed to make a call to Geraldine to say goodnight and let her know of the procedure ahead.

At ease now, the day had passed and the need to rest was with me. Gently I drifted off into a deep, surprisingly good sleep.

Days seemed to roll into each other, and crazily they passed so quickly, I knew the first stage was due but didn't know precisely when, of course this frustrated me a little and with the hunger and thirst I was beginning to feel a little anxious, then there was a knock, a man introduce himself as the anaesthetist, he explained the procedure to me in great detail and asked for me to sign the necessary paperwork, as if knowing the guy I stood up shook his hand, patted his should and calmly thanked him. His smile said it all. "I'm in your hands now thank you" I said and walked the corridor with him. Why did I feel so confident? The whole situation was as though I were dealing with people I'd known for years, everyone around me was on my side, it felt truly humbling..

A group of individuals form all walks of life were coming to me, talking to me, expressing compassion and oozing warmth, this was keeping me going, pushing forward with a great body of people behind me.

Hours passed and still no idea of time I went for a walk, up to the coffee shop upstairs, it was fast approaching closing time and I knew the food would be put away, no fear then that I would buy something, I sat in the window, the view was stunning and people below were scurrying in the streets in between cars and buses they meandered, seeming to all be hurrying, for what?

This recently was a question I often asked myself, what is this all about? Life...

The answer was so simple, as life was itself, we made our own way, create our own destiny through our choices and actions. Life was easy it us who made it complicated, materialism and the want for more took over, to give our children what we never had was so important, and the powers to be knew this and capitalised on it through the media networks, branding and consumerism that was engulfing the easy things in life, keeping up with our neighbours, friends and family had created so much bad feeling that the power to want had taken away the need..

We had lost our way, looking over the city I could see so clearly how we had fallen prisoners to our own desire to have the best.

Who cared really?

Just sat here in this place, I felt it all, care, compassion and friendship so evident that it made me cry, there and then I felt tears rolling down my face, these people didn't know me , didn't judge had never even seen me before were helping me through this surreal and painful time. Mostly they wanted for nothing but a thank you or a smile, that's it a simple thank you.

How humble is that?

Just imagine doing your job, loving it and expecting nothing but a thank you in return.

This team here on ward A800 and the surgeons too were exactly this way.

Returning to the ward, I must say, after tea had been served I was met by my brother Stephen. Beaming smile and pat on the back we walked back to my room, the conversation was a mix of humour and seriousness alike, Stephen and I had a good relationship, both of us had lived a little and shared some fond memories over the years. As with all brothers there was a true sense of being, a team that came together in times of need. Admirably we could stand tall in the knowing that this held us together. At times we had our differences and like in any situation through life, it takes time to sort itself out, we both knew that.

Time passed and Stephen had to go, he had a bit of a week ahead and would try to get in again soon. He reminded me that I should call mum from time to time just to keep her updated. Parting as he got into the lift. We shared a hug goodbye.

The sunshine was beating down across the rooftops of Bristol and I sat gazing once again towards the hills in the distance, incredibly the heat of the sun warmed my face and I sat with my back to the sun for twenty minutes, really absorbing the comforting heat..

Calling mum at about 8.30pm I asked if she'd been to see dad at all, Helen, David's wife had taken her as all the boys were too busy was her answer. No one felt the need to tell dad and mum felt it wasn't really a good idea as he was in his place and although he was a little confused at times he still had positive thoughts, mum had also been to the spa with Helen for a little pamper afternoon. She loved her little treat days made even more enjoyable with a glass of chilled rose (nanny calpole as we liked it to be called) at the end of such, how stressful mum? As always mum was laughing at the end of the call and we said our goodbye.
I'd promised everyone that I'd update them daily through social media and what a task I'd endured upon myself. Sending messages over the media, I copied and pasted lots and a few were repeated, some with kisses and hugs were forwarded to people they shouldn't have been but what the hell, everyone I needed to know knew and I felt that's all that mattered. I had to

be hard on myself where friends were concerned, as I knew many types of people loved to assume, I didn't want any negativeness entering my world at this time.

After a brief chat about the procedure and the signing of various papers with the anaesthetist I was deemed ready for the laparoscopy procedure, butterflies were in my tummy, and I felt a little bit scared, or should I say unsure of it all. I listened to some lovely pieces of music that had always helped me in these kind of times, I adored the sounds and works of Ennio Morricone, his compilations were mainly composed for films and he had a very unique and distinctive style, combining the voice with the instruments, almost using the voice as an instrument, I just loved his work and it helped me.

My brothers Paul and David had arranged to come over later that day as we were told the whole thing would be a couple of hours, after a warm shower I changed from my own clothes to a surgery gown with a tie up back, basically bearing my behind to the world.

I sat in the chair and stared at the clock, watching the time pass by, I loved time and how it made us all equal, no matter what we had in possessions, health, wealth friends and family the one thing we all had was time, an equal amount of it too, every second, minute hour was the one thing we shared.

Music softly playing in the background, the sun through the window, tummy rumbling, I was in a good place as the porters arrived to take me to theatre. They were considerate in their movements as I hopped onto the bed like a gazelle, looking at me in amazement, as I said " I'm only ill on the inside guys."

They chuckled and we proceeded through the ward to the lift, the nurse was walking with me and asking the usual things about life, what did I do, where was I from? Of course this is their way of relaxing us before we arrive in the room prior to the operation.

Surrounded by red gowned individuals, all being caring and doing their thing, I was asked to put a mask over my face as I felt the drowsiness come over me, I could hear the voices as I felt myself drift off to be with my horses at the land.

Coming around, with a song in my head, I began to sing in the recovery room, the place was filled with people busying, doing their stuff, patients in all different moments of recovery and little old me singing away, a red gowned figure approached and held my hand saying the lovely words, " well done Simon that was well done." I hadn't done anything but apparently I'd done it well..

After about 45 minutes of my singing and chattering to myself, I was taken back to my room on A800 room 30. My brothers were sat there as I returned and greeted me with smiles and hugs, I felt ok and enabled myself to get on the bed, I sat up in the bed, tummy bloated, and asked for some water, my mouth and lips were so dry and I wanted to gulp down the glass but the nurse advised me just to wet my lips for a few more minutes.

The three of us chatted and resumed our brotherly banter as if nothing had gone on. It was 5.30pm and apart from feeling a little pain, discomfort, I was also obviously swollen in the tummy maybe even a little puffed up, I was ok in myself when they left, the whole afternoon had for me been a success. I drifted in and out of sleep for the next few hours and the nurses occasionally came to see me, I managed to get up with the aid of them, just to get to the toilet and brush my teeth too, I tasted this metallic almost putty like sensation in my mouth and asked what it could be.

"The medication would certainly be effecting you, in my opinion." said the nurse.

" I think you're doing really well Simon, keep going." The other commented.

"I'm on my feet now and I'd like to stay focused on doing things." came my reply.

I was always determined and had an inner strength that at times seemed a little stubborn, I guess I'd had some many occasions where I'd have to go that extra to achieve what I wanted and this had stood me in good stead. I was after all a doer, who thought beyond thinking about things to just get on with it, I led from the front and had the ability to raise my game when needed.

A great attribute that some admired and others were jealous, envious of, many people saw it as arrogance and made comments to others about it, funnily enough they never said it to me.

In my opinion this then became more of a problem for them than me, what was said about me behind my back was nothing to do with me, nothing to do at all, none of my business really.

Longing to eat I managed to try some cornflakes, wow! They tasted good with the cold milk soothing my somewhat dry throat, feeling more than happy with my day and the teams efforts I called Geraldine and wished her a goodnight.

My phone bleeped at 7.15am, it was from my lovely lady wishing me a good day and letting me know she'd slept ok. Immediately I called her and she was thrilled as I sounded more awake than last night. I'd slept through and had been woken at 5.30am for observations, then blood samples taken straight after.
It was the hospitals way of waking me, a quiet knock to the door, then entered the assistant nurse armed with heart and blood pressure monitor also the thermometer, which was inserted into the ear for a second or two before bleeping and registering the bodies temperature, all amazing and so advanced, on

occasion though the nurses would also do the Obs manually. The old method of hand pump and stethoscope with the upside down time piece on the uniform for them to count the seconds. The reliability of machines was crucial, there still being the need to have it checked manually was also deemed to be decisive in accuracy. Strange in such times of advanced technology.

Breakfast was served at 8.00am, tea, toast and porridge were on my hit list, also a nice shower and tidy up before doctors rounds, I liked to be in my clothes when they came in, it gave me the feeling of normality, simple but true. I walked gingerly around the ward as the soreness of the incisions, be they only small were quite painful and I still felt a little bloated. Managing a couple of laps I was happy to return, sit and read one of my accumulated books, I had a few here, Stephen had brought in an autobiography of interest and Geraldine had also came in with a few, my preference was autobiographies as I loved to know more about the true times of people than the fictional stories they told.

McQueen was at hand when the consultants came in, I stood to greet them shaking their hands in a gesture of welcome,

"Good morning." I softly said, as they observed my movements.

"Good morning to you too Simon." came a reply.

"Good news on the procedure, it was very positive and we have good things to tell you, the main thing is that the tumour is localised and there are no signs in the surrounding areas, we flushed and washed the area with saline and all is as it should be, you'll be going for a further scan today or tomorrow but be assured everything is as fine as can be. I'm very pleased with the findings."

"Thank you, thank you so much, so localised means in one place, yes?" As tears welled up in me, I was so emotionally charged at that time, I couldn't wait to tell people, the need to scream from the rooftops was brewing….

Localised……**LOCALISED**….

Elated and in need to share my feelings, the team left me.

Straight away, picking up the phone, I called Geraldine shared the great news. My thumb was sore through texting all my family and friends the findings of the day.

In times of need we find true compassion in people who don't really know us, some of whom have as much if not more trouble in their lives than one could ever imagine, not that they show it or feel the need to expose you to it, they just are there, a smile, eyes that don't lie, listening with no sense of judgement, true samaritans, these special ones seemed to be all around me at present. I felt liberated by them one and all.

Fact was I had a tumour in my body, an alien causing me considerable pain and at times discomfort, obvious too was my yellowness. This had been determined and had to be dealt with, we needed a plan, I know the medical team were ahead of me already and had the next procedures in hand but it was me, in need of a plan a most definite route of attack. I spent the next few hours organising little achievable goals for myself, strength and nutrition had to be in there, so too had to be one's mind. Positivity lined the walls and listening to one's

emotions decked the halls. My pieces slowly fell into the puzzle and I had a great sense of being about me. I knew that at times I would be tough, hard to myself, an island with no lighthouse, however I'd keep going.
Strutting the wing for the umpteenth time that day, I just knew we were on the right track.

Days in hospital rolled into one, same things happening, people coming and going, patients constantly in and out, this may seem odd but I had managed myself quite nicely, making the whole thing better than my imagination would let, I felt positive and wanted others about me to draw from my wealth of being, feeling confident in ones actions gave light to the healthiness of the mind. We as an intelligent species could let our mind run ragged, even more evident in a situation like this, hospitals, institutions, places that enclosed you could make one feel a little cut off, almost imprisoned to a degree, therefore the mind could empower such.
Imagine being held in a place against your will?

Knowing that if you left or walked out you would be vulnerable, get scared or even become a victim of your own choices. Would you?

The choices you make, lead to actions you take, resulting in the consequences and responsibilities that your life's cycle brings. This said, being aware of your own sense of responsibility can open your eyes to acceptance, and blame, for one makes the choices but rarely can one accept the blame. All that happens in your world is down to you, very rare, if not ever should one blame others. Most definitely we have become a blame culture, thus giving way to the lack of respect we show. For me however, being in here is a necessity, a need for me to be well is important too, both to me plus all those around me, I have a respect for myself that I treat people in the way I'd like to be treated, honesty and trust is felt firstly in oneself, without either how would we know the way to show others such attributes. The staff and people in here show all the meaningful things that make the days seem so bearable, time is given, care is considerate and honesty along with integrity is displayed in all they do, from the first moment I stepped across the threshold of A800 I was part of this family, this team of do unto others. No doubt in my head, looking forward was the way, people here were together harmoniously in all they did.

Two days had passed and I had recovered quite well from the laparoscopy, almost to quick really, but typical of me I was raring to get on to the next stage, it was Friday and obviously I knew from the signage upon my door that the procedure wouldn't be today, no NBM gave it away. Just tests and more tests, plenty of nutrition and fluids to build me up to the level required. The consultants had been in and confirmed to me that it would most probably be tomorrow now.. I got straight onto the networks and told everyone, who ever would've imagined, me being a whizzo on the communication front, here I was thumbs and fingers poised for action, yes using two digits, even three at times, Wow!!
People who mattered knew, that's what was important to me.
Those who matter, care and those who care, matter.

Another unforgettable but meaningful saying that rang true in life.

Many times I had heard or even created such things, more often staying with us for reasons that not even we could explain. Adding to my belief, thinking to much about something means we will over analyse, missing the trail of thought completely, as quite often that thought would lead one away from the reason we had that thought. Overthinking, leading to complexity, it's a fact that life is easy, it's us who complicate it.

Paralysis through analysis....

Friday, visits were over and Geraldine and Ollie had been in, Ollie had known me more than anyone of my friends, we'd had some incredible times together over the forty plus years of knowing each other, we'd laughed, cried, ran riot on occasion and even exchanged words of frustration with each other, still came through it all with a friendship that had grown year to year, sometimes we'd pick up from where we left off with such ease that honestly it could've been yesterday, if I needed a friend, I could rely on Ollie, finding him sometimes was a different experience but he'd be there, on it once he knew. I loved this man.

I walked with them to the front of the hospital and we shared a few minutes on the roadside before they set off back to Bath.

Geraldine text me when she got to her mums house, Joe was patiently waiting there in the window when she arrived, she said.

Geraldine still had to get to the horses and put them to bed with rugs, feed and waters topped up for the night before returning home, to tend to her and Joe's needs.

A long day once more for all, I surely felt it as I turned back the bedclothes for the night.

I slept through, only having a couple of calls of nature.

What a week that was.

Saturday and the weekend was here, Geraldine was attending the horses and coming straight over as soon as, I'd had breakfast followed with a couple of cups of tea, awaiting the doctors rounds, I'd already had my shower and was fully dressed as if expecting a day out, feeling great in myself I took to having a chill and kicking back before the day really had started for most, it was only 8.30am,, most people weren't even with it yet. No excuse, I walked down the corridor through the large double doors and into the sun drenched passageway, it was really welcoming as the sills to the eighth floor window were just like seat, deep and comfortable for me to sprawl myself upon, soak up some sun and forget about life for a while, face was a glow and boy did I feel alive, nothing seems to make sense when I look back at it. Here was I, in hospital with a life threatening tumour, had just had a big breakfast, showered and was now basking in the spring sunshine, not a care in the world.... As if...

Looking across the rooftops of Bristol and out towards my hometown of Bath I was drawn to fluttering wings on the adjacent roof, some fifty meters away, it was a nest of gulls, mother poised over the nest, and three chicks appeared to have hatched somewhat recently as they were very tiny, mother was somewhat frantic in her quite evident protectiveness, squawking, pacing and wings flailing in the morning sun at anything that seemed a tad to close. I sat, amused for a few minutes by this most natural take on life, a rooftop in a large city that was home to not only the patients in the hospital but this new family of gulls now too. It did make me love life even more. The horseshoe shape of the ward meant that I as a patient could only travel one way therefore not missing anyone who entered or departed, advantageous for me as I could always hear footsteps of people and determine the difference between the sounds of these footsteps, you see nurses and patients wore soft footwear so did the physios etc, the cleaners and housekeepers always had trolleys so they squeaked, or at least their trolleys wheels did as they approached, where as the visitors were quite often in harder soled shoes as too would be the consultants, so I'd hear the clicking of the heels against the hard floor, we also had the surgeons and doctors in clog type rubber soled footwear that squeak in a definite manner. Like the eek! Of a mouse. How could hospitals be boring when the mind lets you create games, like identify the next passerby? I was never going to be a normal kind of person, with a mind such as mine, who knows, whatever next? Creativity and imagination were my doings, as I've said before I was a doer not a great thinker.

The sun in my room was above the tree line and to the rear of the building so yes, I moved the table and couple of chairs, benefitting myself by being able to see the trees and blue skies when eating breakfast through until the evening twilight. As I altered the room there was a tap to the door, entered one of the consultants, I liked my team and this man was to me a direct and honest individual that I admired very much for his professional and sincere approach, I liked the way he shook my hand and greeted me, his sincerity was impeccable, his honesty priceless, he spoke with me for a few minutes, again filling me with confidence and focus on our teamwork I asked him if there was anymore I could do to help myself. His words were simple and meaningful, not for any other reason but for me, he asked me if I would like to go home for the afternoon, maybe even the evening, as long as I retuned by 4.00pm the next day, my eyes welled up and of course my answer was yes, the feeling of confidence in his words filled me with both strength and humbleness.

"I'd love too." Came my reply.

We walked to the desk front opposite my room and he informed the staff nurse and nurse assistant of his suggestion, in agreement they all wished me a happy evening and get out of here came from someone, thanks was easy and I stood there for a moment before finally shaking this mans hand in gratitude of being so compassionately understanding, within seconds I was again on the phone to Geraldine with the fabulous news.

Outside the hospital the land rover drew up and Geraldine was greeting me with that smile, throwing my bag across the rear seat I leant over and Joe was there, strapped into his harness so he couldn't jump on me, his face was beaming with excitement and his whole body was waggling in happiness...

Happy to be whole again, our little family spun around in the road and began our journey to the land where the horses were, our little piece of heaven...

It felt so great to be as one again, we were a true unit, in our element in the old landi defender too, it trundled along, every pothole and discrepancy felt through the big old wheels, yes it was a big old lump but it served us well, we used it for both towing the horses and trailer to working as a tractor across the fields, through the woods, it would get us anywhere we wanted to go, just a little more time was always needed, we always carried provisions on board, snacks and coffee, bags of nuts and fruit, of course little Joe knew this and would often guard the centre consul by sitting over it, his head between his legs and paws firmly securing his wares. His eyes were fixed into mine as I talked, his head rolling on his legs as if he could understand all we were saying. Such a lovely boy, and he knew it..

After about an hour of driving from the busy city, we indicated left for the last time, finally there my heart was thumping excitedly. Drawing up to the gate I stepped down, and exactly as predicted they came hurtling from the bottom of the field, knowing the distinctive sound of the Landi and maybe could even smell me.

They flew across the bank and like a true herd they came to the gate skipping, bucking and bunny hopping in excitement. Nothing new there, Yorkie was head of the herd followed by his entourage, typically Jaffy followed up at the rear, keeping his distance and showing his excitement from afar, he skipped and spun on his hind legs, showing us his agility and prowess, even at 24 he still had it..

In fact they all had such presence, I stood at the gate for a few minutes, admiring, just in awe of them really...

Geraldine got out to undo the gate and I walked into the yard, proudness came over me as I knew the feeling it gave us all, we had created this place through our hard work and determination. It certainly was great to finally be here again... Looking to the skies, I gave thanks to the consultant and just knew how good this was for me.

Geraldine caught me wiping a tear from my cheek, knowingly no words needed to be exchanged just a hug, "come see, come see," she said.

Like two teens we held hands and skipped toward the manicured front garden of the old lodge, obvious someone had been busying, tending to the garden as well as doing the guys, truly a marvel, it just showed how much it meant to us both.

Breathing in the air and seeing the gorgeous garden with the blossom and new life coming to all the trees and flowers was incredible, I felt alive once more. Birds song filled the air and pheasant, rabbits and the resident buzzard pair made it more special today. It's like they had all come to see me this afternoon. The horses made their way over too, they knew we were here for tea and to put them to bed but they wanted to wait at the narrow gate into the school, they were fixed on what Joe and I were doing, Joe was chasing his ball in the ménage, jumping over the poles scattered around the school, I said to Geraldine,

"why don't you get tacked up and have a ride? I'm here and it would be great to see you enjoy it."

"You sure?" Came the reply.

"No time like the present babe, giddy up."Almost taunting her into it.

Within minutes the horses were stabled and Tiep was brushed and prepped, just needing his tack and Geraldine her boots and hat, no turning back, the rider and mount were well on their way.

It was great to see Geraldine ride Tiep, really enjoy herself and him too, they had a bond and deservedly so, the work had been put in and benefits were at last coming.

We finally got back to the flat in Bath at about 8.00pm, I was famished, so too was little Joe, he knowingly had taken his posture up next to the kitchen table, eyes upward in my direction, I could almost hear his little voice saying, "chicken and veg dad please?"
Hearing doggy voices were part of my hunger regime too.
"Feed me now…."
I could eat anything and Geraldine knew it, we had steak eggs and salad, with beetroot and spring onions, vegetable pizza and fresh fruit.
Food fit for a king.
Running the bath and finally relaxing at about 9.45pm we finally had time to speak, time for us.
Short-lived even then, Joe needed to go for a final walk before the daylight diminished into darkness, Geraldine told me to just stay chilled and relax in the warm candlelit bath.

Upon their return, I was found under the duvet in our big bed, Joe in his fear of missing out, freed himself from the lead and hurtled towards the bedroom doorway, scurrying around the door, leaping onto the bed, he was there. Plonked in the middle, like he'd grown there. My lady took her bath and joined Joe and I in the large warm bed, family all cosy at last, we talked a lot about things that mattered and some irrelevancies too, it seemed we had a lot to say but mainly we felt the need to just hear each other, finally I felt myself drifting off to sleep.

The noises of the night woke me a couple of times, people in the street below and the cars and taxis passing through the busy city at night, laughter and calling out was commonplace as the moon got older, in between the hustle and bustle was the silence of this town, so quiet, like I was asleep but was I? So different was this town during these hours as by day it was hectic with traffic, honking of horns, people, phones poised, buses the constant hum of the day, but at night you could hear the heartbeat, smell the people as they displayed their rituals of happiness through veins filled with life. Sleeping was easy here even amongst the cries of the night.

Waking up to the sounds of the bells ringing, birdsong and Joe's scampering was definitely a something I had missed so much, Joe and Geraldine were off to the park for walkies before travelling out to the boys for their breakfast and turnout, I called out as they were leaving, reminding them that my favourite breakfast was poached eggs, tomatoes, spinach and smoked bacon on sour dough toast, yummy!

"I'll get some on the way back." she said, as she kissed my cheek on the way out, "now just rest up, I'll be an hour or two."

Gone like a flash. I heard the main entrance door slam in the wind, looked from the front window as Joe skipped along the high pavement towards the park.

Reflecting in the large sliding wardrobe mirror I could see this man I had come to recognise, drawn in the face with a yellowing to the skin and eyes, I pulled back the covers to reveal how much of myself had gone, the weight I had lost was incredible, I wasn't some one who had a weight issue anyway so it came as more of an impact to me. Inside I could see me, through my eyes, I was more than there, the need to smile

came over me, within a flash I was aware of my presence shining back at me, lifting me, managing to bring this moment to its pedestal once more.
I poured some coffee, sipped.
Wow!
That hit the spot.
Scrunched up my hair, pulled the strangest of faces and was out of bed, to the bathroom, a flush and a brush, ice cold water splashed to the skin, eyes smiling back at me I turned to the window and let the lungs fill with the Sunday morning spring air.....
I was me once more....

Key in the door, "hey we're back," came the call, followed by,
"You ok love?"
Still in bed but sat up reading, as I heard the bag of groceries hit the table.
"Yep, all good thanks just enjoying being, you know."
Kettle was on and I could hear the bread being sliced across he board, the flat was alive again, Joe was chasing his bowl, now empty of food around the boots and shoes strewn under the

kitchen dresser. His little furry stoat toy was next as he hurled it into the air, parrying it away with his left paw, then vigorously shaking it in his teeth. He loved it, as we all did here, it was our home..

Sitting at the round table in the kitchen, window wide and city in full view, we took our delicious breakfast, perfect even down to the last mouthful of toasted sourdough and jam washed away with good Italian coffee, the words were still few but heartfelt, it's how Geraldine and I were, we spoke a lot, well at least I did, Geraldine listened. Most seriously, we were able to talk about all and sundry, we had no distractions here, no TV, Ok, a radio that came on occasionally and sometimes her ladyship would buy a magazine or snoozepaper.

We talked, and laughed with not a care in the world, our boys and girls were happy in their horsey world, Joe's life revolved around all we did and we wanted for nothing, we'd earned our pleasure and deserved our way of life..

I washed the dishes and made more coffee as the bath ran for me, soon we were to head off back to Bristol. We stopped off in the village up at Clifton, just taking an hour to walk the streets, people watch and fill in time before returning to he hospital as promised for about 4.00pm.

We pulled to the side of the road and I hugged, kissed my beloveds, painfully stepped from the landi trying to avoid that moment and walked into the vast hospital foyer.

I arrived back on the ward on the 8th floor, Sunday afternoon between lunch and tea, walking the horseshoe shaped ward to my room in the far corner. All exactly as I left it, my heart felt a little flat and for a moment I was alone with thoughts of emptiness.

I missed so much already.

Dropping my bag to the bed and unzipping my coat threw an air of resignation to our situation, back again, revitalised, ready to get it on, and now we had more knowledge, much more factual awareness, the time was upon us...

The next few minutes were in slow motion, I walked slowly from my room almost wanting not to be seen, towards the lifts at the end of the corridor I stopped and perched myself at the rail, watching the newly hatched gulls as they raised their heads, beaks open awaiting food from mum or dad. Amazingly the feeling of life filled my veins causing me to walk on, tall and sharp in my stride, I scooted onto the ward acknowledging all as I passed along.

Afternoons, were exchanged, pleasantries too but most of all eyes and smiles filled my world once more.

Sunday evening seemed to pass quite quickly and I had now the use of my brother Paul's tablet, mainly to watch sport or the odd film, he'd kindly put on a few films and channels that he knew I'd like, also I had obtained more reading material from various people, I loved autobiographies and true stories, basically just because they were easy to relate too and always expressed truth, cookery books and travel were also amongst my library.

A fine selection to while away the long hours. Tonight I took on the new book in my collection, the biography of one of my life heroes, thanks a lot Mr Kibblewhite, My Story by Roger Daltrey. I turned in early, knocking out the first hundred pages in no time, I finished the weekend with a goodnight call to Geraldine and Joe...

Tomorrow was to be the start of treatment and I needed that rest I'd had over the weekend to kickstart the days ahead. My phone bleeped a few times with good luck messages from both family and friends, these messages gave me feeling of magical support and I felt the strength from everyone as I drifted into a deep sleep. The nurses looking after me tonight were in to see me, taking observations and blood tests, making sure I felt happy with the future plans and telling me of the up and coming days, it was the most amazing nights sleep I'd had for weeks. Feeling totally refreshed as I woke to the tap on the door, the young nurse greeting me with a big smiley hello, blood pressure heart rate and temperature taken I was informed that I was to be NBM from 6am, eek! Better have a drink then, she returned with a nice cup of tea, strong and hot and so welcome. It went down a treat and I got up almost immediately afterwards, being 5.50am I turned on the TV above my head and watched the daily start to the news. It was the 20th May and as I've said before I didn't do news or media so this was just background for me as I prepped for the day, I took a long shower, brushed my teeth and sat astride the bed for half an hour, many a memory and thought ran wild in me and I felt safe, really at ease..

I dressed, put on my flip flops and as breakfast was being served I needed to be away from the food, I hated feeling hungry, or as Geraldine so often reminded me hangry, I got quite temperamental when food couldn't be had, after 3 laps of the ward I took up my phone and messaged Geraldine, just letting her know I'd slept and that I would call in a moment or two. Few more laps later, I sat, called home from the window and shared the story of the chick gulls and how I'd watch them from day one, hatch, grow and call for their breakfast.

Procedure was definitely going ahead today, this afternoon in fact and I'd got into my gown ready for the off, time seemed to drag and my nerves were beginning kick in too, butterflies were something I loved and adrenaline rushes too, so I just got into that mode of the excitable unknown before going off on the trolley, arriving at the radiology soon after 3.30pm I was introduced to the team involved, they all paid me undivided attention and reassured me through chat and banter, it seemed to be a place of ease, not at all daunting, and everyone was so inspiring in their attentiveness. A local anaesthetic was administered and the surgeon talked me through the whole thing, continually asking me if I were ok, if I had any questions or queries, also giving me the chance to view the images on the screens. Truly amazing, these people were incredible, all this going on in my body and they just get on with it, all the way through making sure I was comfortable and confident.

All over in no time at all, back in the recovery suite, surgeon and team gave me the thumbs up and I was told all went well, given a drink of water and an hour later I was back in room 30. The days work was a success.

Back in my bed I felt tired and groggy, very hungry but not in need of food, more a drink, my mouth was dry, tasting of the medication and anaesthetic, yuk!

I may have spoken to soon but I was feeling it now, totally in pain, stomach felt like it was going to explode and I couldn't breathe properly, what was happening?

Doctor had had a bit of an issue getting the drain in and needed to be a little forceful thus maybe causing an irritation in the area of drainage. The pain was excruciating and my body was cramping up, more drugs were administered and the nurses had called the doctors up.

I'd messaged Geraldine and my brothers previous to this, telling them how it had all been successfully achieved and how happy everyone was, the way I was feeling now it certainly had changed in me, tears were beginning take hold, my emotions were running a mock, all I could think of was Geraldine and Joe, staff were working with me, calming and reassuring my thoughts with touches of sympathy. I felt the need to tell Geraldine but didn't want her panicking, how was I to do this? I needed to calm myself. Just sent a note to brothers via social media explaining a little about how I'm feeling, as being sick on occasion, hopefully that will help them through the night but I'm feeling lousy and don't feel I need to worry anyone at present, it's getting close to 9.45pm, time to phone and say goodnight, I'll make it quick and easy on us both if I keep it short.

That's the way to do it, fully understanding as Geraldine always is, I'm happy in the knowing that at least she is in bed at home, oh! I can't tell you how much I miss you babe..

My positivity is keeping me strong and I know I'll be able to sleep soon, it's what is needed, good sleep and rest, my mind needs to drift away somewhere, just be free of this and I'll sleep, I know I will. My breathing changes and I relax in my self before dropping off.
I manage to sleep for a few hours, before the pain takes over once more, this time I'm feeling totally out of it, not knowing what to do is one thing but not being able to explain the hurt is another, please someone, please take this from me. I pray that my voice is heard, looking to the skies outside, in search of a resolution I feel my body sweating in anxiety, my hearts racing once again. It lasted for a few more minutes before the nurse came in to do observations again, noticing my anxiety she talked to me in a soothing and calming tone, making me breathe in a relaxed way and generally nursing me through it all, I had more pain killers and this along with her attention seemed to ease my panic. All the time my need to talk was taking away the uncertainty in me. Feeling totally

shattered to the point of exhaustion they had to calm me with drugs and whatever it took.

I was now on self induced morphine, maybe this was affecting me? Was I just panicking or was the pain really that bad, I needed to rest, sleep more, not being in my own head scared me, I lacked control albeit I was in control of the drugs, I was scared, terrified.

I tried to call Geraldine, holding myself back from revealing too much, her and Ollie were going to pop over later that day and I just needed to get through it, best way possible.

Ollie and Geraldine arrived and I was completely out of it, they were polite and so good to me but I knew, I could tell from the eyes, it couldn't have been easy I was in a mess, they had to leave, I had to get myself out of this hole, I was sinking fast.

The next few days were oblivious to me, I had pain like I'd never felt, then vomiting, breathlessness and a swelling in my guts that drew my breath through the hottest of coals. How much pain was a man to take?

Cold sweats and violent shaking followed that night with more attention given by this incredible team, where had these angels come from?

Who knew the reasoning behind all this? Incredibly they never left my side and aided me through with love and tenderness, not at anytime showing any let up in their duty of care.

"Simon are you ok?" I heard across the bed, "can you tell me where you are?" The voice was clear and totally at ease, concise in fact.

"I'm in hospital the BRI in Bristol, why?"

I could make out the clock on the wall opposite it was 4.15am and I watched as the second hand passed the 12, such relief fell over me, the clock was ticking still moving forward, that meant I was still ticking, moving in the same direction, a strong breath filled my lungs and I exhaled, the erratic shaking stopped and sleep came to me once again..

The consultants had agreed that maybe clamping the external drain for a day or two would bring the internal one into more of an effective state, this was something that had raised the bilirubin levels and the evidence was clear in my yellowness to skin and eyes.

Pancreatitis was the diagnosis, I had developed this ugly but very painful complication, it needed to find its settling point and I had to deal with it accordingly, more pain relief and more treatment, if anyone was wanting to take my hurt could they please step up, I'm ready. More visits from family and friends were happening and Geraldine grew in stature, her resilience was totally rocklike, she knew what to say and more importantly when to say it. I sometimes had to pinch myself, my world was full of people who cared so much, friends and family alike made easier by these people here, my new family, a desire grew in me to be there for them too, inspiring me to lift my head high and march on, picking up on their strength I continued my fight.

Messages and calls came to me, friends found out and came forward, strong in support, making the days pass as I built my strength, This was a battle and didn't I know it? For the weekend came upon us and it struck again, more pain, sickness and this time the need to scream, I can't do this, my heart is pounding, lungs burning, cramping in my chest and guts with burning across my back, more nurses, more tests and medication and the doctors once more in attendance, my time was falling away from me, almost being torn in half, I wanted to cry, needing a hug, locking in only on one persons eyes, I could see the pain, the fear, no way was I ready for this, falling to my knees, the urge to curl up, embryonic like crept over me and so I did, my trousers were tightening, guts burning, my bodily functions took over my relief was astonishing, within seconds no pain, no pins and needles. My hernia had somehow popped back into place and the relief was unbelievable, I managed to stand to my feet and walked into the bed area, to everyone's astonishment, the words were easy, immediately I said "the pain had passed, I've no cramps at all, and I've managed to relieve myself of the trapped wind."

One by one they left my side to leave me to more tests and observations, the doctors needed me to have an ECG and maybe a scan first thing just to make certain of my state. The next few hours I was monitored and given pain relief. It's on nights like this that we just got to learn to trust and work as one. No man is an island. The need to tell all, to confront the fears with others is so evident in these times, bottling up doesn't deal with it, prolonging it more like, bravado is foolish when it comes to ones mind. A problem shared, is more than halved, put it out there for all to see, let all around you help you, take advantage of their wealth of knowledge, their understanding, it's your pain, share the hurt and your body will ease your mind as the mind eases the body, after all you are your own bodyguard, you are the most important person to you.

Determination drove me to my feet the next morning, I sprung from bed and showered took my own clothes and walked off ward to the upstairs restaurant, the city morning was busy on the streets and people were hurrying to their places of work. I took a black coffee in a China cup, tasting was so different to cardboard ones. No sugar, just the kick of the caffeine. Rolled back my shoulders in the chair and chilled to the world below me. People came and passed as I enjoyed my time there, finally I picked the moment and was off down the stairs to the ward. Doctors were on rounds and I was told that I was in need of more investigation, firstly I needed to have an echocardiogram, a check of all muscles, valves and action of the heart blood flow etc. This was done by a young man from Portugal, he talked me through the whole thing showing the moving images of my heart and valves etc, advising me that he could see no concerns himself and all seemed well, this was reiterated to me upon my return to the ward by the consultants.

Relief is such an understatement, another step forward, my bilirubin levels had again become a concern as they were fluctuating daily, the clamp now removed and drains flushed regularly seemed to periodically alter the levels but it was still not enough. I again attended the radiology dept much to the enjoyment of the team there, they made it so much more than a procedure, they actually had fun with me, laughter eased the anxiety and concern, this was so evident here in the BRI, it was a remarkable place , all departments making you feel confident and comfortable.

The porter recognising and engaging in conversation as he wheeled me off along the corridors once again, "had I watched any of the football?" He asked.

"A couple of games, it wasn't bad, I like the respect they gave the referees and officials, what about you?" I asked.

"It's soft though isn't it? Really not true football, some pretty players though, but women and the World Cup well I don't know."

Eighth floor and the door to the elevator slides open, back in my room within a minute or two. I raised myself onto my feet and stood as the staff flocked over, intrigued to see me. It felt good to be back amongst the people I'd come to know as I said farewell to the porter.

It continued from there really, the drain had been successful even though we'd had a flare up of pancreatitis but the antibiotics and medication for pain had helped in the settling of this. More investigations were needed and undertaken as to why the flow of the drain was differentiating daily, the internal drain alongside the pancreas didn't seem to be as active as the drain to the external bag, that even at times seemed to slow, causing an issue for any further treatment to continue. We had come to a stale mate and the whole team were baffled as to what to do, this was most seemingly evident in their actions over the next few days. I was left on intravenous antibiotics 4 times daily and more blood, urine and stool samples monitored. It certainly didn't alter the attention and continued support I was receiving from both the ward staff and the consultants, not to say Geraldine my family and friends too. Days past that soon flowed into weeks and without these people about me, well I just don't know, the staff showed concern if they had not seen me walking the wards and quite often one would come to find me, just to see if I was ok, on numerous occasions the ward sister would send me or even bring me a shot of espresso, always have a giggle for ten minutes then be off doing her thing. Everything they did was directed towards my concern and welfare, it's incredible how much we have the time to give time but never do, and here I was, at times feeling fine and happy in my days with this formidable family around me giving me so much love.

In times we say we need friends to be there, alongside us, to guide us through, this was certainly a time for more than just a friend and I was seeing people in totally different ways and feeling their strength to a much enhanced level,

Words were expressed by phone, in text messages and on social media, mostly though the difference was shown through the wanting to be near, everyone even with their own busy lives would just show up, engaging in chat and banter, bringing joy mainly but showing love in their eyes. It was so evident and at times very moving to be part of it. Often I would be sat there or walking the ward when suddenly a familiar face would show up, unannounced and not for long but they would just bring that sunshine to the moment. I felt so special even in the quietest of moments.

Few days had passed and things were seemingly running along ticketyboo as such, I'd been up to the village in Clifton with a couple of friends close friends Ollie and Hobbo, we'd had coffee and cake and had walked for about 300 yards and returned to the hospital by just after lunch when I had what I recall as flareup of constipation, thus causing my stomach to seriously swell, my temperature was high, along with sweats and the excruciating pain I became unable even to cry out.
My goodness this was extremely agonising,

I'd maybe eaten something or done too much, for the next few minutes and beyond I believed I was going to be found slumped on the bathroom floor in my room, the panic chord was beside the shower and the door was ajar to the room, if only I could get to my feet I could reach out for help. Dizziness and fatigue were kicking in, my breathing was erratic,I managed to push myself against the toilet through the door and with all had in me I used the door to get to my knees, then to my feet tirelessly slumping forward to the corner and gasping for air the nurse at her station noticing me, cried out.

"Simon, Simon are you okay? Can you hear me Simon?"

I fell forward and all I can remember was I had a group around me once again..

More work and needles, more tests and time, more love than fear, as they worked tirelessly with me, bringing in more machines and devices to determine as best they could what the hell was going on..

A young lady doctor was at my side holding my hand and consoling me as the others were fixed in concentration, working frantically through the moments to decipher what the issues were. They found that I had both internal drains somehow were blocked, by what they say was a fungus, this had attached to the inside of the plastic tubes and was causing a reversal of the flow of bilirubin, hence the jaundice and yellowing again of the eyes, but why the pain? Pseudonymous another bacterial infection was the new troublemaker within me, more and more waiting, intravenous medications again, leaving me with the taste that I hated, my whole system tasted metallic, oozing a zinc like aura, eyes feeling heavy, tongue swollen, and that disgusting reflux flavour like linseed putty. It seemed steps forwards and backwards were commonplace.

Doctors came in answering the numerous queries and reassuring any doubts, family and friends showed concern and anxiety, mainly as the only true point of contact was me and I'd taken to letting them know everything as and when it happened. Prayers were made, nights were becoming long as too were the day, woken at 5.15am for bloods and observations, IVF to the cannula applied, back to sleep, if indeed possible, the treadmill was taken up daily and I was the hamster. We even tried more exercise with the physio staff getting me an exercise bike in the corner of the room. All was being done that could be, my strength had begun to come back, weight gain was noticeable and my appetite was huge. My pain less and I had been taking fewer and fewer pills. I still had a spring in my step and had lots of fun and banter with all the staff.

It took time but the fact that the hernia was an issue last time and was causing more and more frequent issues made them act with that in mind, one consultant in particular, was at this time planning I had my drains flushed once more and then the main procedure could follow soon after and they were deciding on dates, it looked favourable to go for the first of July, radiology on Monday 1st and later that week the operation to hopefully remove the tumour and infected areas of the liver. We had a plan, a date was in place and the whole scenario had a sense of finality. The microbiologist came to see me in person and give me more of an insight into the goings on inside the drain system that was infected, his explanation of all and the fact that the antibiotics needed to be changed once more indicated to me that all was in order and we were very close now. He gave me an insight into the fungus and its ability to get in the way, block procedures was the reasoning for delay. More work from all still had to be done the nutrition and exercise regime was well underway, nurses and staff on the ward were in full understanding and the surgeons scalpel was in hand, all now was up to my strength and ability to get fitter both physically and nutritionally, plus get rid of the infection causing the rise in bilirubin. Almost there I could see the finish post, so near, yet still a few steps to overcome. These were some big steps. Good news always recently seemed to be followed by issues, I didn't feel the need to build myself up and just reiterated everything as said by the team back to both friends and family.

Visited that evening by two friends was a real treat for me, we'd worked together and had had many a laugh, socially too. Sladey was a full on, in your face character with a heart as big as

life itself, he had the belly to match though. His work ethics were legendary, if I'm holding a brush I'm either sweeping or painting, and by Christ, some of his cutting in was as if he'd used a yard broom, tea was the only thing he'd give real time to, his favoured words would be often, "Come on, come let's get a cup."
Followed by shshsshh a whistling from his lips that were divided by that tooth. Yes, that tooth. He'd quite often put his index finger to his mouth as if to express quiet, I'm sure it was to check the fixing. He was a great guy, with as I say a heart to match. Hobbo on the other hand was a friend I had known all my working life and we'd shared a lot of fun through both bad times and good. He was always there, never to busy for me, as most people felt that hard to believe, they tended to think he was hard to get hold of, never had I experienced this, sure sometimes a bugger to work with but still a good friend, and had I noticed it more recently, he'd had a few health scares recently, few issues that brought an air of inevitability into his life. Work so much, wasn't so important and the need to please all had finally dawned on him.

We had both been in business a long while and had seen, heard and endured all the trades customers and excuses. In fact we'd used most of them ourselves. Besides all this he was a good mate, caring and compassionate.
The three of us giggled like kids in the playground, thus doing me so much good, laughter always would bring me up, certainly it changed my perception of things. This was all about me now and I knew it, but they knew how much it meant too. We walked to the lifts, doors closing they were gone.

Saying goodnight and sleep well to Geraldine and little Joe was easy that night, we both were tired and the words were few but heartfelt. I longed to be close, cuddled up, as my love did also. Slowly I drifted away to that place we all love to go, that little place in our hearts, if you count back from 10 I'll meet you there.

Within these walls there was definitely the most beautiful way about people, tremendous success amongst such consideration, everyone had a job to do and it was incredible to watch the team balancing all the balls. Mingling bodies

all and everyone, collecting information to obtain the correct solution and alas with one person in mind, the patient, my welfare, I was so important to them. So when the consultants teamed around my bed once more, I knowingly had made myself aware that whatever they say today it could differ tomorrow. One man spoke out and told me the thoughts of their meeting earlier, "we have come to the conclusion Simon that it would be best for us all at this time to put off the main surgery, try to reduce the infection by removing the external and internal drains and inserting stents to try to aid in the cleansing of the liver. Do yo understand?"
I thought and nodded in understanding.
He continued to go through the reasons and explained if this was successful that maybe then, and only maybe the hernia could be done too this week.
"Are you ok with that Simon?" He asked.
"Yes, totally." Came my response.
"So two procedures this week, both to give me a better chance to get stronger, yes?"
"Of course, I'll come and go through it with you latter part of the day if that suits."
That said they all left as quick as.

Another change, more sense was my feelings, I let everybody know the news and sat digesting my new way forward.

Later that day the consultant armed with files and papers under his arm came to my room, his smiling face and keenness was my kind of friend, I loved his positivity, moreover his eagerness to draw the diagram showing the procedure, an ERCP. Endoscopic retrograde cholangiopancreatography, yes, it involves passing an endoscope down into the intestine to diagnose disease in the biliary system, pancreas and liver, it will look upstream where the fluids come from to determine the best surgical procedure, it is not considered a dangerous procedure but is not without complications, he explained all this in a very detailed manner and told me why I needed it. It was to insert stents into my liver to drain the bilirubin, basically an internal stent, sounds simple but I can assure you that's because it was explained so well, I was in awe of his ability to just tell me. So I would have internal not external drains passing directly into my lower intestine. Also if this were to be without complication they may have the opportunity later in the week to repair the hernia, yes all in a few days, "how do you feel about this Simon?" He asked.

My reply wanted to be ok if that's it then let's do it, not me I paused looked at him, staring straight at him I said, " I'm all yours, in your hands, thank you so much.

Why I said that I'll never know, I just wanted to get ahead for once. The past few weeks had seen me go through so much and I just felt the need to start really fighting once more, I felt good and we had a real plan of attack.

My smile filled the ward as I walked my laps that evening, all the staff noticing I had my mojo back, wondering why too, I told who I felt I could share it with on the shift that evening, each of who were thrilled for me, as in they shared my happiness. I too shared all with friends and family. I told everyone over the next few days and to my surprise they were so happy to be finally moving in the right direction.

On Sunday the morning was filled with joy as it was my birthday, yes I was having my 55 birthday in hospital with all my adopted family, of course my real family and friends were coming in later and we'd have cards and cake together but it was 6.00am and visitors weren't ever here much before lunch, even on this my birthday.

I donned my flip flops, flowery shirt and shorts and escaped to the ward, skipping amongst rooms and singing to myself along route, I was on a floating cloud, my very own magic carpet. No thing or person would bring me down, today of all days. My dancing feet were drawing attention, my swagger was evident. Lap after lap before finally I came to my room and sat there like the cat who got the cream. Within minutes of sitting the happy moment of the morning came to me, my lovely Geraldine, followed by Hobbo my good old friend, Geraldine came in with, yes, a large chocolate birthday cake, cards and gifts from her family, we all shared the next few hours of the day exchanging laughter and smiles before Hobbo left, soon after my lovely finally made her way off to the lift with me in tow, she had to get back to get Joe from her mothers before going to the horses for their feed and turnout. That time already,I took my lunch, a Sunday roast with pudding to follow I had this overwhelming feeling. An hour passed, it seemed the staff on duty that day had a surprise for me, a rendition of happy birthday, truly unprepared and totally eye watering as too was the big fat chocolate birthday cake, if I didn't have health issues I sure would after today, it was huge. The guys were all there in my room nurses, sister, nurse assistants, cleaners, and house staff, my heart felt so good I had to jump to my feet and give each one a thankful kiss, male and female they all got one. My trust family here had brought me to tears, a true bond between us all had been set and here I was surrounded by people from all walks of life, all with problems too of their own, however they wanted to share my day.

Feeling so elated by this fantastic gesture I felt I had to share this moment, I called Geraldine and my brothers, telling them all about the past half hour, the joy it had brought into my world. How lucky, yes lucky was I?

Now definitely in need of a siesta I took to the big armchair for some me time , after all I was nearing the pension age now, you know when eyes get heavy mid afternoon, just as I was drifting off my family entered, brothers and mum armed with cards gifts and bits and pieces, no peace for me we chatted for a good couple of hours about the past, our childhood and how we shared so many times, just like today our past had been full of surprises.

Slowly the day was catching me up and my folks noticing this, decided to get on.

Cake and more cake at my side, until the moment that'll be with me forever, I took one cake for the daytime shift to share and the other for the night owls. They deserved it and more..

So appreciative in every way, I had more smiles with the night staff, more best wishes all night long. My birthday had literally been all day.

I didn't even get a slice of cake for myself, no problem though as I was full of love and admiration for everyone.

Morning broke, Monday 1st July. Nil by mouth, on my door, this meant something was about to happen. I was unaware in fact had forgotten with all the excitement of the day before that I was due down at radiology for a small procedure involving my external drain, it needed to be flushed and checked out for movement.

The consulting team were wanting to know why the drain was slowing even more.

The porter arrived at my place at 8.30am and I was whisked away to the radiology once again, greeted by the nurses and staff there most of which had seen me before, I was taken into the treatment room, laying under the large machine, the team all about me as the screen was switched on and the procedure started. It wasn't too long and the gentleman explained all in detail, also pointing to the screen and indicating to me what was happening and how it was achieved. I was done, back up to the ward, and my day was back as normal, exercise and food, more walking and cycling reading and just chilling, unlike the manicness of the day before, I had no visitors at all, not that it bothered me, I had the presents of my friends here always bringing a smile and chatting. At times even coming in just for that a singalong or just to gossip for a bit.

Two consultants attended my room that afternoon to tell me all about the mornings findings, there was an issue, some obstruction had caused a slight slowing of the drains, hence the jaundice was more evident however as I was due to have the stents done this week they were happy to just continue with the antibiotics until Wednesday and hopefully the next procedure would aid in clearing the bilirubin from my system.

Very happy in my world at the moment, obviously I had all these issues going on inside me I felt good, in my mind I was strong as I had a great team about me and between us all we were slowly getting there. Everyone was behind me, giving me strength and it filled me with a massive humbleness, again I thought of how these people treated and respected my feelings and took my world and made it their place to get me strong to get there again, truly exceptional people with compassion in their hearts.

Monday passed and the evening came, I had called Geraldine a few times that day, we had spoken of yesterday again and how it had moved us both so much, she was so reassured in everyone's kindness that it seemed to ease the worry in her voice, as like all and everyone her worries were there, contained in her thoughts, held in her heart like mine were too. She dealt with it. I knew it must be difficult and she knew that my dealings were somewhat selfish at times, understandably so, we were a good team. Our respect, strength and love would pull us together and help us through.

My attitude towards everything had not once wavered, my insight into things was growing through the roof, whenever I doubted I asked the team, never asking social media, ooh! That fearsome diagnostic doctor media. I felt the truth was so easier to deal with and the look in people's eyes could never lie. I had great respect and felt theirs too.

Tuesday arrived with the sunshine and a lovely hello as bloods were about to be taken once more, as they had been throughout my stay here, every morning 5.45am or there about without fail, a sharp scratch and done. Next came my vitals or observations, all seemed fine and I was up and wide awake ready for the day ahead, the exercise bike was always tempting first thing so I gave it fifteen minutes before breakfast, it sort of gave me a sense of earning my day ahead, I took a hearty breakfast three weetabix, two brown toast and marmalade with orange juice and a cup of tea. I could eat, that was for sure, I had a great appetite and loved my food once more. After breakfast I took to my morning stroll and called Geraldine, as I had done every morning I called to fill her in on my nights sleep and see how she was bearing up, she was already at the horses and feeding ready for their day in the stables. It filled the time for her and after she would drop Joe at her mums to make time to see me in the afternoon.

We spoke for a few minutes and I then continued my stroll about the ward, hellos and good mornings, cheeky grins and greetings exchanged I walked my six laps before taking a shower in my room, by this time my bed had been made and room cleaned, I used to leave the music on in there just because I knew certain people loved their music, in particular two cleaners were well into the same things I played, reggae and soul music would echo from the walls and on occasion one could hear a sweet voice singing the songs coming down the ward. It was great to be a part of this and at times we would spend time chatting about music and families as if we had no cares in the world, truly comforting. As music brought us all together.

Once more the consultants would appear with the plans and strategies would be gone over for the days ahead. My comfort was in their voices, so humbling and heartfelt. Our need for full support must've been evident from day one as it grew with each passing moment. One day filled the next with positivity, the desire to get on with things was extremely important to me. I believed they, the team that is, knew this and strived in their professional ethics to achieve the same.

My Geraldine arrived soon after lunch with the usual treat of a luxurious foot massage, giggles and tender moments of affection. Our hours always seemed to pass so quick, never enough time for what was to be said, however we often sat in silence just taking in the moments we shared together. The clock ticked by, standing still outside the elevator we gazed at one another, without words we shared yet another goodbye. It wasn't as written in the romance novels, those farewells upon the screen, this was in real time, a true parting with complete respect and devotion, no need for anything more as we knew how we felt.

Afternoon sunshine filled my walk back, the view was amazing as too was the growth of the young gulls on the adjacent roof. They were as large as their mother now and still looking to her for feed. Nature at its best. I sat and watched them for a good 15 minutes with the sun on my back, smile as always, just happy in my world.

Evening fell and soon I was socialising on the media with my friends and family, telling them the plans and expectations of the days ahead, both of my own thoughts and the team. I called my mum as I needed her to know how I was, more really to help put her mind at rest through the reassurance of my voice and with the laughter we had so often shared. I took to watch a bit of a film, mainly just to settle my thought process really. I knew NBM would be soon and the next day would be spent in theatre and mostly under the influence of anaesthesia so I just kicked back at watched the screen, not really taking it in, more just background stuff.

I woke early with the usual morning routine followed by shower and gown ready for the porters at 8.15am. Off to the surgery and once again the same familiar faces in the radiology dept where the procedure was to take place. Disclaimers signed and forms filled I was walked into a cubicle where I took to a bed before being wheeled into the room. Wow! At least 10 people there and the surgeon introduced himself along with the team on duty that morning, being conscious at this point was really quite strange as normally I would have been away with the fairies by now, it just felt surreal as the guys all introduced themselves I felt the need to say who I was too, this brought a smile and laughter to everyone's face, lightening the moment and as always a touch of ease fell upon me. I soon was under the influence of the anaesthetic and awoke in the recovery room, what eerily seemed moments later, my throat dry and sore but I felt the need to sing to the staffs amusement once again, oxygenate the lungs is all I can recall the surgeon saying to me many moons ago, "sing to your hearts content." As I recall. So I was. And I did for a while I know. I was taken back onto the ward before I knew it, greeted by the nurses once more, I was in my room, sat up and sipping water, I was once again longing to eat but told I had to wait, aaargh!!

Feed me now!

Noticing the external drain had been removed and feeling a little pained I managed to get to the toilet that late afternoon. I felt ok, the tiredness had passed and I wanted so much to eat that I was quite agitated and surprisingly the dreaded 'hanger' was showing its ugly face. I was brought some food, greedily gorging it and wanting more I grabbed a big bag of mixed nuts and devoured the lot. Content or soporific I just full up, I felt the desire to sleep but knew it wouldn't be the best. I stayed awake and spent the next few hours on the phone and Internet, forcing myself to stay awake until I could call Geraldine and let her know the outcome of the day. We chatted and laughed about my carry on within the theatre, it lightened the mood and filled the night with calm and detachment from the seriousness of all.

Goodnight love was exchanged and the sleep fell easy once more.

So far the week was going reasonably well and the last procedure had been achieved according to the consultants plans, now we had a well earned rest day before the next steps had to be performed. Still on antibiotics and pain relief I took to the ward walking my laps once again, awaiting my visitors and friendly banter from all the staff, my day was like all others, full of colour and enlightenment, giggles and smiles. I saw the consultants once more, they gave me their updates and thumbs up, my bilirubin had settled and seemed to be decreasing slightly, all good for me and themselves alike. Things were groovy, going our way. My appetite was filled with a nice big lunch and treats that Geraldine had brought in along with the bits and pieces my brothers had decently not eaten on their visits, I was totally comfortable in my skin. Outside the sunshine was beating down and I knew that it wouldn't be long before I would be part of the real world once more.

I called my friends, family just to hear their voices, listened to some reggae music and read more of my library of books. Ate a big supper devoured more fruit and strolled the corridors before finally settling in about 10.30pm, where had the day gone?

Tap, tap, to the door " good sleep Simon," came the voice.

"Like a log," was my response.

More intravenous drip and bloods taken, the body and mind just accepting it easier by day. Vitals done by the assistant nurse, my day had begun with the early morning call of these angels. Never failing to amaze me with how jovial and smiley they could be so early in their days. Yes, ok, I may have been somewhat of an easier patient but these guys were much the same to everyone, even the disgruntled, argumentative and downright rude people of the ward were treated the same way, incredibly patient, with all type of patients. They had true saint like qualities, one and all.

I was once more NBM from the start of the morning 6.00am was my last cup of tea and I was to have no breakfast either, I'd sort of become used to the fact and knew how to distract myself enough, brothers all helped with the messages of jokes and laughter, also I had the luxury of being able to get on my bike, ha ha a real treat. As I sat there pedalling away in the mid morning sun the consulting team arrived and told me of the days agenda, all being well with my stats and bloods the hernia would be sorted today or tomorrow at the latest, more likely today was the plan. Great news, again my thanks was evident as they left the room to my appreciative smile. Without ado I was on the phone, thumbs and forefingers in full flow as I typed the news to all, I took the next few moments away from the pedals and called Geraldine, her response was one of ecstasy once again, more positive action was being taken.

The relief in knowing that the hernia was due to be fixed gave me the strength to believe in myself even more as I had felt that would be the last of their issues, especially this side of the main procedure. They were obviously happy in my health, albeit a little wayward with the mass still there, however they felt they could fix this before making the move to the next stage. I was honestly feeling and seeing light at the end of the tunnel. My steps were small but forward.

Afternoon was well underway when the porters arrived with my theatre bed, "chariot for Simon." The cheeky one said.
Up I got with gown and surgery socks donned. "Off we go again,"was my remark as we set off once more to the elevators. Riding the lift down was funny as we joked about my stay in the ward, and how long I'd been there, the other porter was amazed by the facts as we joked that I'd only come in to the hospital for the hernia. We had to let him know that we were pulling his leg and this was something that got in the way of my main surgery, therefore they had decided to fix it. Time was fast approaching 4.00pm as we entered the pre theatre room, the staff as per usual were there in anticipation of my arrival, I again met the anaesthetist and this time the surgeon and his entourage. All before the cannula was used once more, as I counted back from ten I heard the laughter and

relaxed way these guys were in control. My eyes were heavy now and my throat was dry as I drifted into a deep sleep. I was thinking how their working days were always filled with all types of people, all having more than the last person. The why Me's and how comes, were so tolerated by the staff.

In the recovery room I woke, although not fully, A sense of outside was drawing my attention, unbeknown to me I was already in a dreamy place even though I wasn't quite awake yet. Come on let the fun begin,
"I tried to catch your attention Spike,"
came a voice in my conscious. It was so surreal, that I should be thinking like this especially as I had just been operated in the last few moments, I was uncertain what was going on. "Where did that come from?" I heard someone say.
Recovery room was a hive of activity, everyone busying around the patients, groans and exasperated lungs were being filled, awakening people all about me, as I again had to comprehend what was happening, the nurse

was tending to me, when suddenly out of nowhere I uttered,

"Paul was due in very soon, Stephen too, you'll have to be quick."

"Pardon me Simon, what are you saying?" She asked.

I had most obviously been dreaming of seeing my brothers and awoke myself in mid dream.

"Did you call me Spike?" I asked the nurse.

"Are you ok? Simon please are you?"was her response.

The bewildered nurse continued monitoring me as I garbled on about things, totally irrelevant to what was happening to me. My stats were good and I had a small drink of water before seeing the clock on the wall and asking,

"Can I eat now?"

All I ever worried about was eating, I'd had surgery and all that concerned me was food. Typical, as my mother would say.

"As long as your bellies full all is ok."

I was taken back to A800, whilst the nurse who had been attending me was still struggling with what had just gone on and my actions, I'm sure.

My room was quiet as I fell back to sleep, the young male trainee nurse came quietly in with the observation trolley, woke me gently, asking so softly if it were ok to take my blood pressure etc, his eyes were fixed on mine as he asked if I felt any pain,

"Only hunger,"was my reply, " I'm starving, bloody starving."

My pain was measured from 1-10 and at this time is was about 3. My blood pressure, heart rate and temperature were all good, it was my oxygen that seemed low as he administered the tube to my nasal passage, cold air hit the back of my nose causing me to cough slightly, the realisation then of my hernia repair. Carefully with a towel rolled up against my stomach I began to clear my throat.

He brought me some cereals, after finishing my stats.

The senior nurse came in and asked how I was, looking at me and studying my movements, asking if I could get to my feet, to try to stand, which I did and even went to the toilet, in a bottle at least. I saw my reflection in the mirror, ooh! I was rough, my skin was oily and hair seemed to be greasy, obviously the bilirubin was still high, causing me to look more yellow than earlier. The fact was I had jaundice, was tired, had also had a bit of a time of it, this week especially was quite a battering and now I'd had my hernia done. I wasn't going to look like my best hey?

After managing to get back to bed I called my Geraldine, lovely feeling also great to hear her voice and reassuring tone once again. She was due to come in to see me tomorrow hopefully around lunchtime, after doing the guys up at the stables. We talked our days through and said goodnight, before I fell off into a deep sleep.

Slept right through and woke at 5.15am, usual bloods and stuff done but today I was allowed breakfast, yes I knew it, fill your boots son, I thought. That I certainly did, I had it all and more, I deserved it, every last morsel. The morning was flowing quite quickly, I had trouble getting to my feet and using the toilet but the nurse was at hand to fetch me a bottle once again. She assured me it was all ok and I had nothing to worry about, it was just the drugs.

The consultants were in quite early, everything had gone well and my levels were falling to their delight as well as mine, seemed the week had gone well and I had good news to share with everyone. All my brothers were messaged, Geraldine phoned and my mother too.
All seemed fine and dandy.

I'd tried to get to get toilet but something was not quite right. Still quite sore and my right leg still tingling I let the nurses know that it felt numb, with occasional pins and needles, they raised concern to the doctors and I was again watched over for a while. I had to use the bottles in the bed again , I'd never done this before today and it did feel somewhat weird. What if I needed a number two, ooer! My thoughts were slightly distracted by this as I heard the trolley being pushed towards my door,
"Bonjour Simon, ca va?" It was the housemaid, coming to clean my room. We always had a little chat, she was from Djibouti, east Africa, living in Bristol with her mother. We chatted in both French and English which amused me and passed the time in a nice way, as if we were not

in the hospital, just chit chat. I had this feeling with all the staff, a true friendly ambience with them all. It made everything so much more relaxing and I felt I could be me.

Geraldine came in just after lunch, I'd managed to somehow find my feet and at least brush my teeth and have a wash, my leg was slowly coming back to life and the tingling was as if I'd been sat on it for a while, such relief.
We talked over general things as Geraldine massaged my feet with lavender oil, we laughed at my rendition of the recovery room episode, the room never felt like hospital to me, we were left alone most of the time, on the odd occasion one of the consultants would pass by, call in and just explain how they felt it was and where we all were. This was so good for us as it came direct from the team, not me trying to explain how it all was. They certainly had our best interests at heart, showing consideration and compassion with the utmost honesty, true direct and approachable in all senses.
Time flew when I had visitors and the two to three hours just went, it was a busy weekend in Bristol this weekend, St Paul's carnival was on,

the traffic would be heavy and my good lady
still had to get across town back to fetch Joe
and then off to feed our herd of lovely horses.
Leaving the room as I was still a little wary of
walking too far she passed through the corridor
and was gone. I'd promised to let her know if
the traffic was bad, using the Internet I traced
her route and sent her a message accordingly.
Traffic good if you stick to the A4 all the way.
Wilko! Came the reply with plenty of kisses too.
She had got back to her mums quite quickly,
texted me and I called her mum on the landline,
just really to say hello and let her know that I
was in good spirits. Rita, wished me goodnight
and handed me over to Geraldine,
"Speak to Joe Simon, he can hear your voice,"
I called out down the line and could hear him
murmuring in the room, he apparently was
looking for a toy to give me, such a feeling of
togetherness came over me, I said my goodbye
and laid back in my bed with tears in my eye.
It's incredible how we are moved by gestures so
simple but most of all without prejudice,
unconditional love is shown by so many,
animals however never judge or discriminate,

more to the point they express through their actions.

Why have we developed a judgemental attitude?

No man is better than me, no person should judge or even be judged, ok if laws are broken then let the law deal with it, but never look down at someone. Treat all as you like to be treated. This is so how I felt here with all these strangers around me, I felt their sincerity, the love, that's how we should all be.

You are the most important and if you have trust and respect in yourself then you can give that to others.

Deceive and the only one that will hurt is you, for the only person you let down is yourself. Given these words and feeling the simpleness of all around me I felt the need to get to my feet, walk to the bathroom and shower, perfect drive in respect for myself and all those about me.

Later that afternoon I had a chat with one of the team, she advised me all had gone well and if in the next few days my levels were stabilising then possibly the consultants may consider letting me home for some time before the surgery to remove the mass.

"This is only depending on your improvement over the next few days, Simon, ok?"

"It's not been fully decided but maybe possible."

Wow! Really, even more reason to spruce up and get going again, flip flops on and I was once again shuffling somewhat gingerly around the ward, greetings and smiles once more met me on my travels, so what, I know it was only 140 meters but it was a start. Rome wasn't built in a day. Self belief and motivation was my fuel, plus the guys here were filling me with gusto, always encouraging and positive, what a team.

Once again it was down to my drive and my body, with the help of the medication, team and family I was sure to get there.

The thrill of being able to share the news pounded in my heart as I reached for the phone to let the world know. My fingers and thumbs frantically put words together, the brain so excited it went into Blah! Blah! mode, actually struggling to string sentences together.

Slow down, I tools myself, slow down.

My phone was bleeping as quick as I could send. Trying to read and write simultaneously made it even harder and I felt my tiredness kick in. Maybe this was my self preservation telling me to just chill, nothing was guaranteed, decisions still had to come from the main consultants. Feeling almost without control I was asleep within minutes. Supper woke me as the trolley arrived with the smile behind it. The Saturday evening came as I took to the phone to call mum, obviously she needed to know how things were and I wanted her to be happy about the fact that I could be home soonish. Mum sounded upbeat and told me that she was intending to drop over tomorrow with David and maybe Paul too, they'd be here sometime in the afternoon, after lunch, was there anything I needed, fancied, always followed. Straight after my elder brother called and said he'd be in too over the next few days, hoping Monday after the morning rounds of the consultants.

The tennis doubles followed the chats on the phone, then a message came in, my brothers and wives were toasting a glass to me over dinner at Stephens, nice for them, a picture followed setting the scene, for me it was back to the tennis as I enjoyed a peaceful couple of hours before night nights and then sleep.

Bleep bleep, messages flying in, early on a Sunday morning, what was going on? Geraldine had sent me a message to say good morning, not just once, in fact four times.. It certainly woke me and when I noticed the time I couldn't believe it, 6.15am on a Sunday, of course Geraldine was up to take flight early, Joe dropped off, horses fed and turned out then off to work for the day. What a woman?
Up now and wide awake as the nurse came in, bloods and drip done. All the usual stuff first thing, this time I was ready and soon after I was in the shower, shaved and awaiting breakfast. I put the radio on, walked a couple of laps passing the breakfast trolley on the way. Ahead of the game once more, tea and cereals with the usual toast and marmalade, well it was Sunday, music playing reminded me of being at home when I was a boy, dad would always wake us all up Sundays to the smell of breakfast cooking and Dinah Washington or one of the croons from yesteryear. My senses were so

switched on I could hear the bacon and tomatoes sizzling under the grill. My dad made a stonking breakfast, full English with copious cups of tea. Pleasurable memories of youth, music, Sunday mornings and brothers, cousins and family gatherings in the air. Within these moments I was able to share my dreams, the things are never as bad as they seem when you know you have the memories I have had, my whole time had been one hell of a great ride, a true rollercoaster of events and time after time I had such fond moments, in love one minute then playing the field the next, sometimes how did I ever keep up I'll never know, so lucky to have had a life like I had.

The day was in full swing, songs and books were in full flow as I was having a typical smooth day, totally chilling as the consultants came in, they were in and smiles exchanged as we spoke of the previous weeks episodes, everything seemed to have gone as well as they had imagined, finally I was on the road, in the direction they had strived for. Levels reducing slowly but surely, hope also that the antibiotics were able to be reduced too, made the day even better.

Mum, David and Paul were in now too, talking of the weeks happenings with me, they also spoke of dads singing and enjoying the music, mum and Roo had made some discs for him of all his old music, my father could sing well and we remembered many a good evening spent with the sounds of partying. It's funny as I'd not brought up my morning to the guys but we seemed to be chatting about he same things. Crazy how life is.

Stephen had called and said he was able to visit tomorrow afternoon which was nice as I knew Geraldine would be here too. A full day ahead again tomorrow it seemed.

When David finally got home to his he messaged me that Mum had had a nice time and felt relieved about my situation, she was having a cup of tea and slice of cake with them before venturing home herself.

Alls well that ends well, sprung to mind as my day drew to a close, just my lovely Geraldine to say bonsoir to then I could see the back of my eyelids once more. The day had gone, sleep was way overdue and I felt the heaviness pull me to my pillow.

Slept so good, really well, shower time now and food to follow, buzzing and full of beans I was on one. 3 laps and twenty mins on the bike, eat your heart out Mr Motivator. I was on fire, new week, I liked Mondays. Now all done with the fitness regime of the morning and still only 10.20am I was in the chair feet up looking out the window, book across my lap, a book of short true happenings in people's lives. These people had actually written about true events that changed either their lives or the direction they were taking, very fascinating to the point that it seemed to have a sense of how I was beginning to see our lives. My room was silent as I gazed from the window, frozen was the moment as a knock to the frame of the open door, it was a group of the consultants and Doctors just relaying the facts of the blood and results from today's findings, all was once again as they wanted, my eyes, skin and complexion were less yellow and my energy levels seemed good, they were looking to take me off the antibiotics soon and hoping to give me the chance to go home, all was dependant on the net few days findings, also my improvement in mobility and strength. This was fabulous news and I was almost to tears as they left my room once again. Had I made such good progress, this said I did feel good in myself and even though I knew I was going to have a major surgery soon I was overjoyed.

Geraldine came first that afternoon, followed by my elder brother Stephen and then Hobbo, what a great laugh, I had an hour of foot massage and treats with her ladyship, at one time the nurse came in to do my stats and laughed at he attention I was receiving from Geraldine. She was in awe of how my feet were being soothed and caressed as I just laid back chatting and talking to Geraldine telling her all the great news before Stephen came in,
"Look at him, lording it, two women in attendance, lucky sod," he implied.
"I'd like to remind you dear brother I'm not too well here, ok?" Came my response.
With that both the nurse and Geraldine stopped gazed at one another and raised their eyebrows. No words needed saying. In fact the

actions were enough. Stephen and I knew our place as we made light of it and greeted one another, the next hour we all three chatted, mainly of nothing in particular just about our horses, the stables and the plans of when I finally get home, we had lots to say but the time and the place seemed not now as I was so evidently on a high, after about a good hour there was another familiar face in the room, Hobbo had arrived, Geraldine had to go as time was passing by, we shared a kiss, gone like the wind. Leaving boys to be boys the banter flowed, first about footie, then golf, work antics then silly chit chat, us men could be worse than a gaggle of geese, we loved a gossip, many ears were melting that afternoon.

Time flies when you are having fun, this day no exception, feeling exhausted and ecstatic with the moment I curled under my covers like a kid in his den and called a few people to say goodnight, finally falling off after the last IVF drip was set up. It hopefully would now be the last one. Yes, I'd hope so!

Tuesday was here, why is it when you know your date of discharge is imminent, your sleep pattern changes and things start to become more difficult to handle. I knew this day would or could be soon and had done so for a bit of time however I really began to feel anxious about the next few days, I seem to change in my way of dealing with things, I felt the need to tidy my head, clear the mind of all the things that would stand in my way, I started to think of getting the grass cut and school rolled, why? I was really finding it so difficult to come to terms with. Maybe even a little institutionalised. I had been here for three months almost, it could be this, maybe I was afraid of not coping or failing Geraldine and family at home. Could it be that I felt safe here? Sure of all about me, that it gave me a feeling of security, I'm not sure but today I was certainly in another place...

The day dragged and I could feel the dryness in my throat as I tried to speak with the nurses about it. They were so supportive of my reasoning and truly understanding of my situation but not once did they or anyone judge.

"You'll get there Simon, wherever it is you'll get there." Said one nurse in particular.

This brought me back to reality as I knew that I needed this day to come soon, for all my desires to come home to me. I was far from stupid, knowing how it felt meant I could deal with the questions in my head. I could only and should only get over them one at a time. Easy, just take it one day at a time.

Reality was in fact very healthy and I expressed this to Geraldine over the phone.

We'd been through a lot together and even though apart, our strong attitude towards it all was a testament to our loyalty to one another. Strength comes from good foundation and when things are being hurled at you from all directions you batten down the hatches and ride the storm. Stand strong to fight on.

We were strong, listening to her voice made that so clear to me...

One of life's greatest gifts for us all is love, be it from one person to another or solely to love life itself. We all have it in us, so show it, go and tell people, how you see things in love is so different. We lose sight of the truth, through the things that matter least, the material things don't give you love, don't care about you, that's why they break down, not like the naturalness of love, I know love between people fails, falls apart, but deep down it never leaves you, we move on like nature sowing the seeds of love once more, as the mighty oak, standing majestically proud, it blooms every spring, comes back to life every year. Nature is pure love, bringing to life every spring the place we love and live in. Anger is emotion, love in fear of being lost, most of us get angry through frustration of love and how it's misunderstood. It's because we care so much, are losing our way, frightened that the one we love is misinterpreting love. Hold onto love, anger is like the falling of the leaves it's natures way of being angry, the autumnal storms of nature along with winter blow the leaves from the tree, the bear hibernates in the cold of winter, only from time to time does it rage like this but the natural world still is alive with lovely things about us, the snows of winter, the rivers that flow unto the seas that sometimes rage, those fluffy clouds, some dark some white, with rain like tears of nature but come the spring when the darkness is over, it brings blossom, its own way of rekindling love.

For reasons my feelings were being echoed in my head as the day seemed to drag, not in a bad way, just slowdown a little. I knew what I had to do however I needed this to happen for me to realise how lucky I was, I had it all and more, with more to come too.

Feeling much better and it's only 11.45am, my visit from the consultant team was same as, hoping that I could be home on Friday, levels were still dropping, bloods showing good, and my stats were strong, lovely for me to be able to share with everyone.
Paul thumbs up, Geraldine a big yahoo, David is over the moon and off to my nephew Charlie's graduation in London, so double celebration for them, Stephen's congratulations were for both Charlie and I, all in all only Roo to respond but he was with Mum seeing Dad at the home today, thus sending me photos of dad, videos too of him singing and listening to his music, like father like son. Friends and family all informed of the same, also the friends here were hearing

the good news and it made for a happy time amongst us all, sharing is caring and these guys were as much a part of my family. Every step taken was forward in our eyes, my colourful shirts reflected our time walking the wards, they doing their caring and me doing the sharing, smiles for miles and miles, I had my team behind me all the way.

I'm not sure where the time went after lunch, as I chose to kick back and relax with my book, thoughts were good and my time was spent catching up on some me time, I thought about seeing Dad and Mum, my lovely Geraldine and the horses, Joe my little mate and my brothers, I could hear the sound of hooves across the yard, smell my dog, hear the banter of my family and taste Mum's fresh biscuits, I wasn't even home yet. I was drooling though.

Unlike the morning the afternoon flew by, tea was served and with belly full I strolled out to view the seagulls nestling in the sun, the sun was over the hills, hiding behind the majestic clouds from time to time, causing the shadows to change from each building below. The city unlike here was bustling, tiny people from up here were making their journeys home to their loved ones, I dreamed of my day soon once more, sleep in our bed, Joe at foot or shuffling the duvet before resting into the cushioned footboard. I couldn't wait, my heart was beating, counting the minutes with every one closer, lifted, I felt absorbed in my life on the other side of the distant hills. Reaching out, I could touch them through the glass, see the Westbury White Horse beyond. Soon real soon I'd be home.

Walking more made easier with the change of staff, hence more smiles and well wishes, the clanking of the tea trolley, or one with squeaky wheels, before making my way back into room 30, my home for the past couple of months, my lovely little place of R&R… I'd become quite attached to my retreat and loved the set up with the Physio's bike in the corner, borrowed laptop and flowery shirt collection. Home is where the heart is and mine for the time being had been here. Showered now ready for bed, and totally in the mood to sleep I found my way between the sheets quite easily. It was still light outside as I felt my eyes fall heavy and I knew I had to say goodnight to my love. Time to call I think, most definitely a good time, Geraldine could hear my tiredness and understood the reasoning, we exchanged our much felt affections with love down the line...

With great sense of being the day was sprung upon me, usual start to the morning, I'd had so many needles in me over the past few months, my arms were like pin cushions, all for the good of myself. We had the normal start to the day and I was ready for the bike now, before I took breakfast I had in my head 20 minutes or so then a couple of circuits, best laid plans and all that. I managed 15 minutes and a phone call to my beloved as I had a missed call, nothing distressing just for Joe to hear my voice before going for his walk in the park. He'd sometimes would roll over on his bed and refuse with quite threatening growls that came to really nothing but snarls of refusal, you want me up then come get me. Ha! Ha! I can see him now, curled up in the big black bean bag awaiting that moment of movement, just seeing the whites of his eyes and teeth bared at you, collar on with lead, poised for the attack that never came. All mouth and teeth that's Joe, he would jump at his own reflection...

Phone bleeps and messages flying in from brothers, tom toms are up early and sharing their plans for the day ahead.

Paul had been up in London the night before seeing his daughters and sharing a pint or two, Stephen however was in a jovial mood sending jokes and dittos as such, I knew David and Helen had the graduation of Charlie to attend, Andrew was silent and had been for some days now. My breakfast was delicious and very plentiful, but I'd earned it. Food was going into me a real treat and I was gaining more weight. I began to feel the benefits of the nutritionists advice so too the team of physios and their input was excellent. I loved how it had made me feel and gave me the drive to get up together for myself. Weight gained through both good food and exercise was important to my efforts, with the right regime our plans were achievable and I felt the need to be in the best shape for the next procedure. All my team thrived on my energy filled inspirational attitude, the better I am the easier it is for you. The consultant and his team made it clear to me daily. I kept my side of the bargain and did what they asked, more at times. I could often feel their knowledge and gain

empowerment from it, almost as if the more I knew, then the harder I could fight. Really drawing from the whole team at times.
I did admire how we were….

Being deep into my book as the consultants arrived with the results of the tests, bloods and levels stagnant, you could see their eyes watching me as I drew energy from them all, the bilirubin was to be the aim now as they told me about my medication changes and if successful then home Friday. Antibiotics altered and now orally managed made life easier and I was almost free of the cannula. Little steps but large advancement. I felt great. Out by Friday with a fair wind ahoy! I could smell the fields and taste the air.

Off I was on my next walk this time I attempted the cool staircase down to level 2 where the shops were, the stairs behind the elevators were cooler and less busy, steep stairs with a full length glass window overlooking the central area of the wing, I took my time, gathering more thoughts about my life ahead, stopping halfway to just catch my breath and fill my lungs with the cool air I noticed the birds outside, fluttering in the summer breeze, out of the hot sun they chased the bugs through the air. Summer brought the smiles to the faces of everyone, the corridor out of the hospital was full of people coming and going, sunglasses evidently on the ones just in from the bright outside. That big yellow ball in the sky brought so much to our lives.

I bought myself some juice and fruit from the shop, engaged in conversation with the young man behind the till, we joked about how people changed as they entered the hospital, he brought a smile to my day with his response.

"They come in here and it's like they have all the worries, people on the wards are the ones with the illnesses, but most of these are visitors, moaning about how they can't find things, crazy world"

My sentiments entirely, don't bring it with you, put it in a place, that on occasion you can bring it out and digest it a little, life is for living without regrets or blame, your choice, your chosen responsibility.

Goodies under my arm I was on the return journey, six floors to walk or take the lift, the corridor was my decision time, as the doors were adjacent to each other, if the lifts were imminent I would ride up, people were milling about at the foyer before the lifts and I arrived as that informative ping sounded on two of them, doors open and like mice we made our way to the chosen floors. Patients, staff and visitors silent on a journey.

Sat in the room with music playing, the sound of the lunch trolley was heard from afar, I was famished as always, mind you I had just been to the shops, returning with bananas, I'd scoffed two, was contemplating the third when the bell went. The little banana was saved by the bell, my hunger needed to be saved, as too, thirst was part of the issue. I'd been drinking so much that I was filling more and more bottles daily. Lunchtime came and went when suddenly through the door came a consultant, with a quick update that the antibiotics were working ok and my levels were dropping. That was that and gone on his travels, continuing his quest of well being.

Lunch over and more time with the inner me, deep thought as I walked with meaning now, my head was in a good place and I could now sweetly enhance the rest of my body, gently

filling my lungs and slowing the monuments ahead down, the path had been laid and a sense of calm was within, no rush, anxiety or need for frustration, just little old me filling the echoes of time with simple thoughts of life and home. Within these walls I captured strength from everyone, as I knew the truth about my situation and felt in complete harmony with the facts. Most scary things to a lot of people, truth normally is however I had an air of serenity within my being that made things light up, don't ask me why? Or how? But I was whole...
Living as me was easy, no doubts no regrets no fears....
Remaining hours passed with few messages from friends and family, all is well that we know is going well, obviously people were awaiting the news that I was returning home therefore were hanging in there with things to say in case it was said wrong, I understood this and reiterated it with every message that asked if we had any idea yet. People didn't know what to say, I made enough noise for all of us and kept as high as I could but I'm sure, in fact I knew I had a little excitement in me, it was

scary, surreal maybe even doubtful but we all knew how much it meant...

Saying goodnight to Geraldine was hard this evening, difficult to find the best way of saying the words, almost impossible to be the one who was in control, this came across as healthy to me as it gave me the realisation that our caring side had to almost shut off to the happiness of one another and become self driven to get our goals. Almost self focussing on getting it right. After saying goodnight my phone rang and it was Paul, we spoke for about ten minutes, in general about nothing but shared a chat that brought me back down to reality and helped in my dosing off. Last stats done now and I was soon to sleep, with the door ajar I could hear the busyness of the ward and see the silhouette of staff as they ebbed and flowed between patients. I watched the shadows and the pillows warmed to my breath as I drifted....

Rat a tat tat came the knock to the door, wiping my eyes I saw 5.45am, blood taken and smiles exchanged, I'd slept well, with more in me I knew and after observations were done I was curled up and off only to be woken by the trolley hitting the wall outside as water jugs were dispensed. Morning had broken and breakfast was on its way, I'd not heard how my duetting partner was and felt I needed to ask someone. It had been a few days and no news, I hope she was ok? I missed the singalongs we shared as my room was cleaned, the little catch ups and her cheeky grin. I know I had plenty of other friends here but when someone is ill and you don't know you tend to think more about them. I hoped she was ok? She'd had a few moments and had trouble at times but we always had a smile and song for each other. I missed those moments.

I was feeling top drawer and felt the goodness inside me, taking photos and sending them to the boys was fun, they enjoyed them as said in their replies, jesting that homers gone and that's not our brother was fun for me, it filled the levels back to the top, so inspiring a few extra laps and minutes on the exercise bike... Paul had seen dad and let everyone know, I'd had a late chat with the Doctors and they said I was well on route for tomorrow, all I needed was the green light from the consultant...

Whenever one is aware or wanting something Father Time always slows, people move differently, clocks tick louder and decisions never seem to come. My world was in sloth mode, bud em bud em bud em!!! As the trolley passed for lunch, same with afternoon tea and supper, even the cup of tea seemed to take its time to cool enough to drink, why???

Like last day of term at school, poised I was, ready to pounce into life, I had one more sleep, or so I hoped...

Last message of the day to my brothers would be sent, it was only 7.30pm the place seemed deserted, even though the silence was in my head as the staff were busying in the other areas of the ward, other patients apart from me were important too, it wasn't all about me, selfishly I wanted it to be, as expected I suppose, we all would...

No news is good news rang inside me, Doctors and consultants long before had gone and still no answer as tomorrow, last update sent to all, hey! Maybe tomorrow?

Geraldine and I spoke and she told me I sounded a little down and I should get over myself, perk up, I'd come miles and to think they envisaged you coming home this early, you'd only had the hernia last Friday along with other procedures in the same week.

"Stop carrying on at yourself, it's time when it's time Simon, you've been strong and now they need you to be healthy and sure, stop being so hard on yourself, it'll happen when it is time." Her words echoed after we said goodnight and I fell into a sleep for an hour or two, woken by the male nurse for midnight medication, he asking me if were ok? Reassuring me with the same enthusiasm as Geraldine....

I watched something on the iPad, I don't know what but it amused me for some hours, well at least until sleep won the fight.

Blood taken at 5.45am, was a real alarm going off, my arm was not even awake aside the rest of me, it had been done and stats were being noted, heart and temperature was all good and I was ready for the days events. Early call to my beloved at 6.45am was brought forward with the excitement that I maybe home, she was off to work today and had already left with Joe, having to drop him over to her mothers for the day whilst she worked. Also early as the horses

couldn't feed themselves so that was another little chore on route for her. All in all what was to be a 8 hour shift at work would in fact be 14 hours by the time all was done at the end...
And I had been moaning in here about dragging hours and long days..
So selfish was I..
My stomach was calling out, even though it wouldn't be for at least an hour, in need of distraction I hopped on the bike and did a quick 6000 metres, then a few laps of the ward. The day shift gang had arrived and I drew the odd smile and hello, Friday and everyone was busy, plus it was still rather early and I was in full swing as opposed to their just starting out on their day.
Getting back to my room I'd had a missed message from Steven, typically a rather good joke, in video format, nice and soft start to the day, brother Paul was enjoying it too, he was off to shoot a round of golf today and was already on route to the venue. I promised to keep them updated on the news and for obvious reasons, I may need a lift back to Bath... down there for thinking, I hear one say.

Over the course of the next anxious few hours we exchanged many a text, joke and brotherly banter, aiding in passing time for all of us, breakfast very soon ran into mid morning and and still no answer, junior doctors and a consulting team came in and said that they were happy with my progress, nurses had rumoured I was on my way but no sign of the main man to give the big sign off...

Lunch came and the fish and chips were as good as ever, unfortunately my thoughts were elsewhere as I swallowed the last mouthful, was it to be today?

More text, voice messages and a call from Geraldine too, reignited the excitement and frustration within me, I had all the numbers in the lottery but had lost the ticket, I knew I had them, here somewhere but just missing, I felt if I left the ward I'd miss the answer, even to walk the corner became hard. Then out of the sunlight on the corridor lit up by the large sundrenched window they came my way, the nurses, big smiles and eyes filled with joy, heading in my direction,

"You're going home Simon, going today, the consultant had agreed and all we are awaiting are your meds and discharge papers, well done you, time to get ready."

They simultaneously said, in fact I don't know which one did say but they were both there and I felt it came from everyone.

"Really can I, really I'm going home?" As my arms flung around each of them in celebration of the moment.

I got packed up in a minute, there were three bags and little old me in my room, my home for the past few months, sat astride my bed as I began to feel the reality kick in. Feeling the need to share it all I called my brothers for my lift home and spoke with Geraldine, the tears flowed down the line as we knew I had finished this somewhat surreal part of the journey. Many ups and downs, sideway steps and swerves but we'd got here and the fact was this incredible family I had around me had helped me all the way, I felt totally humbled by one and all, I needed to share it, albeit with only a few, I was able to say thank you, have a moment with each of them, quite emotional and sometimes tearful for it meant so much as they did too. Everyone knew as I took my bags from my room, the young male nurse aided me in getting them downstairs to meet my brother waiting in the foyer.

I left the ward in complete awe of these angels, everyone a true friend, caring and compassionate, truly inspiring angels who had been a big foundation in my knew life's direction by just being themselves and going above and beyond, my head held high as I took the lift to the 2nd floor, where the young trainee nurse handed my brother my bags and shook my hand saying,

"It's been so nice for me to have known you Simon, you have inspired me to want to be the best and I will be, thank you, pleasure knowing you."

My eyes filled with tears as we parted with a hug and shake of the hand.

"Oh! I know you will be, young man you most certainly will."

Sunshine greeted me as I left the vast hospital, into my brothers van and I was away, on the road to home. No regrets, just heart filled with strength brought forward with the love of others, my journey somewhat felt easier as we had a bond above and beyond.

Messages and more were flooding in as my phone was bleeping every minute, everyone was eager to know about me and I replied as hastily as I could, David and I had a lot to say too, we stopped for fuel, the sun was warm, breeze from the window was amazing as we steadily made our way across the city traffic, Friday afternoon with the sunshine beating down, schools were just finishing and traffic was building up, who cared? I was with on my way home to Bath, my younger brother was driving me, we were chatting oblivious to all about us. In next to no time we arrived at his house, his lovely home on the outskirts of the city, his lovely wife Helen was there too, a big hug and affectionate smile embraced me as I walked up the steps to the door, through the door into their cool hallway, flicking off my flip flops, feeling the cool tiled floor under my feet I finally felt the feeling I was home.

The next few hours we spent chatting, with me of course eating, lovely salmon, scrambled eggs and toast, washed down with fresh coffee and sweet tasting water with a slice of lemon.

Time seemed to slow incredibly as we spoke of the plan ahead for me, we weren't to sure of too much and I hadn't really read my discharge papers, so all seemed a little vague, there was an itinerary however I'd like so many others was just in this moment, savouring the day.

I'd called Geraldine and she was already on route via her mums with Joe, the knock at the door was soon after the call and there they both stood, Joe's tail said how happy he was to see me and Geraldine's eyes too reiterated the same, we paused before hugging and then the eyes filled with the joy and love.

I was back, family as one again...

David had messaged my brothers and family, "eagle has landed."

All replied accordingly, as families do, my thanks and gratitude were made to David and Helen and we left to get to the horses, out to see the guys at the stables...

Wow! When you know you know. It was great to see these beautiful, ok so I'm biased a little however these horses looked great, totally majestic in stature and movement, my god lady had gone beyond looking after them, they were amazing. We were so bloody lucky. Yorkie greeted me with his usual French attitude, so you're back, hello again, now where is my tea? Whereas the others performed a little for my return, Jaffy expressed his normal tongue in cheek method Timmy gave a display of tiggerish bounciness, Howdy and Chance had a mare moment and Tiep tip toed, spun and skipped his way across the field, all in all a magnificently well timed welcome back by all.

We had more hugs and stood in the garden area of the old lodge taking in this herd of wonderful horses as little Joe my saviour fetched as many little gifts for me as he could muster, old gloves half eaten balls and a tea towel were brought over, his tail expressing his happiness as we took all in…

I felt so proud of all we had and knew how hard it had been for Geraldine, not just in the past few months but the years before too, we had this place, our hands and hearts had earned every blade of grass every ounce of soil had taken its toll, there was nothing quite like it for either of us.

It was our little piece of heaven, now and forevermore.

After an hour or two as Geraldine had chores to do with the horses and they were fed, groomed then turned out to graze for the summer evening, it became hard to leave, I wanted more time here, getting tired and slightly hungry was the final thing to make our day move on and go home, back to our home in the centre of the city of Bath, the gate shut and locked, horses playing in the distance as I looked over my shoulder as Geraldine, Joe and I pulled out onto the busy main road into Bath. The journey usually would take 20 to 30 minutes depending on traffic and timings, this didn't matter to me so much now as like everything else in my world, I'd slowed my process of living to suit our way of being. Driving back through the valley towards the rolling hills that surrounded my home town, clouds forming a fantastic skyline, enveloping the hills and city below, my thoughts wereI'm home, ! Wow! I missed so much whilst away and it brought the lifelong memories, it had made such an impression on me over the years, the incredible childhood through the sixties and seventies then through the teenage years of the eighties, the responsibilities of adulthood, privileged by the friends and folk I'd met along the way. Opponents of rugby, air flight pilots & attendants, all fields and people of all backgrounds, most never met before that became friends along my great path, I'd shared so many memories with smiles and feelings that stay with you forever, seen incredible sights breathed air from all continents, yet this city was my home, a place with a magnetism a draw, back to where I knew, I had spent my learned days, that was my point, for today I was going home, still learning about me, my time was teaching me to decant and fill with more expectation. I was happy in my world and as we drew closer to the large Georgian terraces of Bath, I felt myself begin to meditate, relax as if I'd found my missing pieces of my puzzle. Maybe that's how life was, the puzzle of many pieces, all coming together, it was up to me to fill the gaps. Past the old fire station and home was calling. The grandeur of the terrace was upon us, as we hunted for a parking space, yellow lines were in abundance around Bath, we could park between 6.00pm and 8.00am outside the house, you however had to be very lucky as it was a terrace of 36 houses with only a few parking areas. We'd always joke about people that came into town in the evening, how they were taking the spaces, either frequenting the churches or many eating and drinking establishments, only for an hour or two but showing no considering to the residents who lived there, imagine going to their neighbourhoods we'd say? Pulling up outside their house, curtains would twitch and sometimes you may even be approached in protest. We always laughed about it even in the coldness of winter with bags of shopping and Joe on his lead, we would manage, either one of us drop the other or park up the hills out of town where we came across a space. Some mornings I'd wake and wonder where the car was, on many occasions only having minutes to get to the car before the wardens came, the trusty wardens, they were great, always good for a giggle and basically doing a good but hard job, it was something I could never wish to be, our cities wardens were ok most didn't enjoy ticketing people but they had to enforce it and very often were abused for it, usually by the do-gooder, only dropping off for a second or picking up granny from over there, the worlds full of them, you know who you are?

Hooray! A space outside, in fact right outside, so no long hilly walk for either of us, there we were all stationary, I took a big breath and opened the door, only to hit the high edge of the raised pavement, clunk! Whoops! My mistake as I turned to Geraldine smiling. I had only a week ago gone through a few procedures internally and also a hernia repair but now was home in anticipation of the next stage, the ongoing procedure of the liver resection and removal of the tumour. At least I was home in my bed, eating our food and choices of where or when, if at all I wanted too, yes living once more with love all about me.

Kettles on bath running, the flat smelled of home, my home, where Joe ran wild, chasing his own shadow to and fro, burying toys, leaping from bed to bed, ever since his first day here, little Joe had lit up our lives, ensured we had reason, like the horses they were all dependant on us, loving us as we knew and loved too, a more than great reason to appreciate life, inspiring me to be strong and fight but most of all to embrace every moment….

In the warming waters of the bath, sloshing myself like a child, I could smell the wind through the window, taste the air of the city and hear the night come to life. My good lady called to me that supper was soon to be on the table, culinary delights were important to me as I adored good wholesome food and revelled in the recipes of the world, I could cook and loved preparing all kinds of dishes, Geraldine knew this and nearly always let me cook, in fact it was another little joke between us both that I grew in the kitchen, making it hard for anyone else to be able to do anything. Tonight though was a meal prepared as I bathed, nice aromas from the kitchen filled the air as I could hear the dishes being placed on the table, dinner was served, salmon, on a bed of salad with beetroot and and sweet peas... yummy!

All washed down with fresh fruit juice and a nice mug of lemon and ginger tea.

Contemplating dessert was the next step as we had various fresh fruits and Greek style yoghurt, we gave it a miss though as it was quite late and I began to feel a little tired, it had been a long time since I'd slept in my own bed and the day to had been exhausting.

I crashed out, taking up half of the sofa with Joe by my side, snuggling into me as Joe knew best to do. Geraldine did the dishes and cleared the table before waving Joe's lead in anticipation of some sort of reaction, he was settled in the warmth of the cushions and my body heat, "going to be hard work for you babe," I said. " don't I know it," came her reply, " don't I know it," as she attempted to move him from the couch.

"Growl and snarl, grrr owl," leap gone, was Joe's response at the door to the landing closed shut behind them.

Scampering down the stairs, I heard the main door slam and I was sat alone in the coolness of our home, the wind whooshed through the open windows and on occasion the rattling of the old Georgian frames was the only sound I could hear….

I must've dozed as I never heard them come back in, they were here as I could hear the bath running once again, Joe was lying next to the tub and Geraldine had the candles burning on the side with the trickling water at her feet. I took to the seat in the window and we chatted for a good half hour, the water continually ran warming the air, the candles flickered in the small breeze as the night sky changed and stars lit up the vastness beyond, soon the city hills silhouetted the sky, laughter echoed from the bars below, I retired to the bedroom, followed closely by Joe, toy firmly in his lips...

I woke early on the Saturday morning, first one felt great, no needles or stats just a lovely smile from my lady and hot coffee.

New dawn new day, what have we planned for this fine summer weekend, horses and Joe walk, maybe breakfast at the farm shop close to the land. I was so relaxed, in total harmony.

The last few months had past and the future was bright although I had major surgery ahead I had no real issues in my head and the positive attitude I'd managed with good thought, ability to pigeonhole being the best, I was incredibly happy in my world...

I thought about going to see my dad, in saying so my brother Stephen was on my case, telling me I'd be better off staying away from the home for a few weeks as my immunity was low therefore a nursing home may not necessarily be the best place to visit, germs and infections were all I needed, Paul agreed and said he'd come over to the land later in the morning if I fancied a big boy breakfast, my appetite was good but not for that so I declined the offer and tucked into a big bowl of muesli, crunching on the nuts and slurping on the almond milk. Ping! More messages from friends and family were coming fast and full, support was full on. Geraldine went to walk Joe and do the stables on her own, leaving me to soak up the morning in my own time...

My urgency to rise from slumber became obvious to me in that the sense of time stood still, I listened to music, birds singing, the traffic below in the street. It just happened to have a sound like no other, remembering I'd been in a hospital ward for the past few months, with no traffic, no birds singing just the humming of the air conditioning, incredibly I fell back off to sleep, only waking when I heard the key in the door, Geraldine had returned to pick me up and take me out, no rush though I thought.

"We have all the time we need babe' hey! Don't you agree?" I said.
"I'd like to ride if I could, what do you think?"Geraldine's reply.

She had already this set in her mind and I didn't feel I could even be against it, after the last few months that's the least I could give her, an hour in the school was little sacrifice to me and I would enjoy seeing Tiep Tiep ridden. That's it our afternoon decided we headed for the car and off we travelled.

Geraldine loved it that afternoon and I think Tiep was happy too. Our time in a nutshell, spending it among the things we adored, my brother Paul came over later in the afternoon, mainly to see how we were and also if tomorrow morning I'd like to meet him before going to see mum at her place, he'd pick me up about 10.00am and we could get a bite for breakfast beforehand. A plan set and he shot back to his, his being only a couple of minutes down the road in the lanes behind the village of Norton-st-Phillip. That's the beauty of all the family we weren't to far away from each other, all in the Bath vicinity, making it easy for us all if ever issues arose.

Days followed on through the weeks ahead much the same really seeing family, eating sharing moments with friends and generally living, the tennis at Wimbledon fortnight had come and gone so had the world cup cricket which England managed to win in an incredible finale to a great competition, a true spectacle. All in all some great moments with plenty of giggles. My time was filled with other things too, I had twice weekly a blood test to make certain my bilirubin levels and blood markers were good. This was carried out at my GP surgery in Bath, on Monday and Friday mornings early as possible to free up the day, always taken by the nurses on duty, they would kindly ask if I were ok and if I had any thing bothering me, again being caring towards a stranger…

Waking in your own place may be something we take no notice of, just do, however the simple things we take for granted bring the biggest smiles, the most happiest moments, I can't remember the last time I hugged my pillow and lovingly folded back the duvet, smiling in the bathroom mirror lit up by the morning sun was a simple thing whilst brushing my teeth but it meant so much. Maybe I've changed or even this now has made me realise the importance of being me, I helloed my way through the morning, greeting the everyday things in life, simply expressing gratitude towards the man made and living essentials of existence, why can't we greet the kettle, it boils the water that makes the tea, equally the pigeon sat on the window ledge, good morning to you and yours, everything now had a place, realism that could only be filled with meaning. I know it seems strange to have these thoughts, why not? Some people love their cars, cherish their objects, would sacrifice themselves for their homes and all that's in them, so why couldn't I respect my toaster and show it some manners in a sweet hello?

Chatting about simple life things and how soon eventually after all this was over we were going to move forward, we both had ideas and plans, sharing them was the next step, our dreams and aspirations were still there, horses and skiing, Joe the land and new lodge, all still ticketyboo! The conversation continued for the next few hours, as we ate, we talked, as I bathed, we talked, Geraldine's turn to perch on the loo and chat away. The sun fell behind the hills and Joe was in the park for his night time stroll, I finally was in our cozy bed, the summer heat all about me, no air-con, groans from adjacent rooms, just the night coming to life in the street below. Even after all that had been happening in my world, with all the pain and anxiety we had all been through my ability to switch off and sleep was fabulous, I slept through until 6.45am, ok, maybe I got up for the toilet but straight back off again on return.

Geraldine had slept, I think, not so well, she had listened to me, every breath was monitored, taken with me, I was oblivious to her, totally at peace with myself. I knew from her morning greet, the night had not been sleep orientated, in fact furthest from her mind.

Coffee and toast in bed at 6.30am, the sun beaming across the valley outside lit up the room through the large Georgian window, Joe squeaked and jumped onto the bed, the toast was his first thought, drooling he watched as I took my every mouthful. Nothing in his life had changed much really, Joe had made a full and speedy recovery, his only difference was, why is daddy back? He'd been sleeping in our bed for the duration of my hospital stay, mainly on mummy's side, as Geraldine slept in my usual place, so really he was a little confused. This aside he was into my little Joe, my best friend, loved me unconditionally as I did him. Both coffee and toast was finished, we rose from our slumber and headed for the kitchen, Joe flopped into his bed at the door and I found the coffee pot, Geraldine was already taking her morning bath, early to bed, early to see the best of the day, the sun was already bringing the warmth as the birds and city early risers took to the streets. Being a Sunday the delight for me was the sound of silence from the lack of city traffic, less lorries and buses, most evident though was the lack of people, being on the higher floors the footsteps from the pavement echoed when it was busiest somewhat less on a Sunday, which I found so satisfying….

Only a few days previous had I reflected on one particular day after returning home, it had an impact upon me that needed addressing, the day was so meaningful I took hold of it once more and now felt the need to reexamine it fully. The morning began as above, with us up early and our usual things being said and done, this time I'll share it fully.

Geraldine was taking her bath before work.

"What time is Paul coming for you darling?" Came from the bath.

"Around 10ish, we are off to see mum too."

Paul was so often later than planned but today he was on time, I was on the steps outside the flat as he pulled in.

I felt great in myself, even my energy levels amazed me, I had made the stairs both sets from the flat and also at the Cozy Club where we had a great healthy breakfast. It was so evident in Paul, his eyes following my every move, concern was on his mind, I tried easing the situation with humour and laughter, the eyes don't lie however.

We had a nice long chat and as David had messaged me that Roo was taking Mum to see dad we opted to meet a bit later and I could spend the afternoon with David, Mum was going back there later, Paul dropped me at David's about middayish . At David's the looks of concern were much the same but in stereo,

how was this to affect me? Only I could deal
with it, I would never try to tell someone how to
be toward me, so I turned it on myself and took
the pain in their eyes, managed it and took the
strength and embraced it. Energising their
concerns for myself, smiling made them smile
back, so reassuring with a little positiveness and
so on.

Within an hour Wendy Paul's wife was with us
and we had more chat over coffee, I began to
feel a little tired and overwhelmed with all the
attention, although it was lovely and made me
realise how much love we had, it was rather
tiring. Paul and Wendy left, having to get back
home to see to their dogs, within moments Roo
along with Mum arrived after seeing Dad at the
care home where Dad was. Mum was on good
for, well she'd not seen me in different
surroundings for a few months, Roo's stay was
shot as he had things to do, Mum on the other
hand was in her element, asking if she could
have the TV on as the men's final of Wimbledon
was on, it took over the room and she was
completely into it, shouting at them, totally
animated, front of the seat stuff. I didn't mind

at all at least the attention wasn't about me so much..

Geraldine called at about 4.30pm, she'd finished work and was coming to get Joe in Bath so would I want picking up too, obviously it made it easier for everyone and I could at least get to land with her. Within half hour she arrived, came in for a quick hello, said farewell and off, once at the horses and I took a long well earned nap in the new lodge..

Waking after an hour I fondled in my bag for my medication, a new regime I had in my life. Four times a day I had pills to take, my life had never really been medicated, the odd injury and fall had seen the bottle of pills emerge but I'd never like the thought of taking tablets. Now was different maybe, I followed the prescribed dosage as instructed, friends and family search the alternative ethos but I had faith in my friends in the hospital, as they were still in my heart and eyes looking after me.

What a day.....

Once home we chilled and reflected on the days events, I'd managed the day well and had done some exercise too, ok only walked a few hundred meters but I'd done it.
Sleep came quick and easy after food and a nice soak in the bathtub...

First week being home was excellent, I'd spent the entirety of my time with the ones I wanted to be around, Geraldine, Joe, the horses had brought me back to heaven and my friends and family were dipping in and out of my life, how could I thank them all, I'd seen most of them throughout the week and shared love and laughter, it was a fabulous time and I wanted every to know it, ok I'd been home less than a week and only had surgery 10 days prior. Me well I wanted go have a wee get together at the new lodge and show gratitude to the guys so I sent out a message, telling all that I would be lighting up the pizza oven and BBQ at the land on whichever night suits everyone best, it was an open invitation with the only stipulation being they supplied their own drink...

Well everyone was at first unsure about he pressure it would cause me but I felt great and had plenty of help if needed.

The general consensus was to go for Saturday pm, after 6.00pm in fact, Great a day to give a little back I thought. Quick, check of the English summertime weather and hey ho! Rain on the weekend, whatever, we Brits love the rain. I shared the moment with beloved and got to preparing for some fun.

I loved when we had people over at the land and just chilled with good food and a few drinks, we'd done it a few times over the years and as all occasions it was really a lot of fun, having a facility as such, a place that everyone can just relax with no pressure was good, no electric meant no distractions and candlelight made things more social, I'd light a few fires and we all would just chat. We had on a few occasions lost track of time and the weather outside, only to step out from the old cabin, which was warmed by the stove and candlelight, all cosy and snug and find it had snowed in the winter evening, was bitter cold and the place was lit up by the moon and stars, a truly wow! Factor.

Something to take my mind off things is how I saw it, I had a plan in mind, good food and company and the weather was no issue, if need be we could use the new lodge, it was not quite finished but the interior was up together and easily accommodate us all if it rained, food was easy as I loved to prepare all types, it gave me great sense of being, anything that involved others always did. My chores were set, shopping and tidying without exerting myself, Geraldine's beady eye were constantly watching over me, and Joe was always at my side, especially in the knowing that food was about. I set myself small goals as to have time to get it right, inviting the ones I wanted to see, it was fun and took away the stresses of the reality for the moment.

Few days before the big feast Stephen had arranged a trip up to his golf club near Castle Combe, I could maybe go with them and walk a little of the course, he'd also have a golf buggy to use. I met him and we set off, a lovely morning and his future son in law and friend were with us too, the first tee and away we go, golf a popular sport, or in the words of Sir Winston Churchill "a way to spoil a good walk in the country." Ball, tee, club, hole, easy, I'd played a little and found it a great social event with mates, others on the other hand, all the gear, no idea, springs to mind, balls flying through the air, occasionally followed by a stick of iron, even the best of moments could become in an instance terrestrial like, really out of this world, people would physically change, crouching in agony, like John Cleese beating the Morris 1100 in Fawlty Towers, to lifting the Ryder Cup as the shot landed inches from the hole. Everyone knew someone that had moments like these, but that one shot, that one so perfect, was enough to bring them back, the talking point in the clubhouse, the reason next Sunday meant so much.

It was a lovely morning made even more enjoyable with the lunch in the bar after, lovely late breakfast, my appetite has been with me throughout all this and the biggest worry for me would be if I lost it. I filled my belly with poached eggs, spinach and salmon on sour dough toast with extra toast and jam, orange juice, fresh coffee, a kings breakfast and I haven't even hit a ball, still a winner.

Stephen dropped me on route back to Bath, we met Geraldine in a layby at the top of the hills looking over the city, it had been a great morning and I was feeling it a little, tiredness set in quite quickly as we drove out to get feed for the animals. Falling asleep had become part of my regime and I'd do it at times throughout the day, maybe just through exertion but more so because I was ill, I looked and felt well but realistically I was not in a good place. I had resigned myself to live as much as I could and living was what I was all about.

Back at the land, the chance again for Geraldine to ride as the sun was not to warm and the horses were around this end of the field, she loved it, rode well, popping little cross poles and jumps, truly playing with her horse. Washed down and feet done the guys were in and awaiting feeding before we left to go home for a nice quiet evening. Just as we were about to lock the gate my brother Paul showed up, he was on the way back from the gym, he just called in to ask if I was up for an early breakfast again but this time at the farm shop across the way.

"Not too early say I'll come get you for 10.15am and

I loved my breakfast and immediately felt my tummy rumbling.

"Of course great idea, I'll be ready."

Quick hug and cuddle for the three of us, we were on our way home.

Chatting about simple life things and how soon eventually after all this was over we were going to move forward, we both had ideas and plans, sharing them was the next step, our dreams and aspirations were still there, horses and skiing, Joe the land and new lodge, all still ticketyboo! The conversation continued for the next few hours, as we ate, we talked, as I bathed, we talked, Geraldine's turn to perch on the loo and chat away. The sun fell behind the hills and Joe was in the park for his night time stroll, I finally was in our cozy bed, the summer heat all about me, no air-con, groans from adjacent rooms, just the night coming to life in the street below.

Even after all that had been happening in my world, with all the pain and anxiety we had all been through my ability to switch off and sleep was fabulous, I slept through until 6.45am, ok, maybe I got up for the toilet but straight back off again on return.

Geraldine had slept, I think, not so well, she had listened to me, every breath was monitored, taken with me, I was oblivious to her, totally at peace with myself. I knew from her morning greet, the night had not been sleep orientated, in fact furthest from her mind.

Coffee and toast in bed at 6.30am, the sun beaming across the valley outside lit up the room through the large Georgian window, Joe squeaked and jumped onto the bed, the toast was his first thought, drooling he watched as I took my every mouthful. Nothing in his life had changed much really, Joe had made a full and speedy recovery, his only difference was, why is daddy back? He'd been sleeping in our bed for the duration of my hospital stay, mainly on mummy's side, as Geraldine slept in my usual place, so really he was a little confused. This aside he was into my little Joe, my best friend, loved me unconditionally as I did him. Both coffee and toast was finished, we rose from our slumber and headed for the kitchen, Joe flopped into his bed at the door and I found the coffee pot, Geraldine was already taking her morning bath, early to bed, early to see the best of the day, the sun was already bringing the warmth as the birds and city early risers took to the streets. Being a Sunday the delight for me was the sound of silence from the lack of city traffic, less lorries and buses, most evident though was the lack of people, being on the higher floors the footsteps from the pavement echoed when it was busiest somewhat less on a Sunday, which I found so satisfying….

"What time is Paul coming for you darling?" Came from the bath.
"Around 10ish, at the land."
"That's good as I will be at work from 8.30am and you won't be alone for too long up there, will you?"
I didn't mind being alone, in fact it was something I enjoyed at times.
We dropped Joe at her Mum's and made our way to the land, picking up a drink on the way.

It was 7.30 when the guys were being fed and Geraldine had done their hay-nets and stables too. I was in the new lodge just pottering about, clearing, busying the best way possible.

"I'm off then darling." Came the cry from outside.
"Kiss kiss, off to work now all is done, you have a wonderful day and don't do too much"
I stepped out into the sun, kiss to her cheek, and gone.

The next couple of hours I listened to the radio, heard the news and fell back to sleep on the chesterfield sofa, totally chilled.

Paul had come over as planned and we trundled over to the farm shop for our breakfast.
On arrival my phone bleeped and I'd had a missed call from Ollie, he was on his way to see me, I text him our plan and he showed up with Laito his better half. Great to see him and spend time with them all again. Their company was fab, we had no secrets and held respect for each other, Ollie and Paul reminisced about our family and laughed repeatedly, it just seemed so

much easier to get through this painful time with laughter, friendship and togetherness playing such a big part of it.

Ollie and Laito dropped me back at the horses and we had a good hug before they set off to see family. I was completely knackered in all ways, my legs were heavy as too the eyes, sleep was inevitably close as I took up position on the sofa and cushions.

Waking after an hour I fondled in my bag for my medication, a new regime I had in my life. Four times a day I had pills to take, my life had never really been medicated, the odd injury and fall had seen the bottle of pills emerge but I'd never like the thought of taking tablets. Now was different maybe, I followed the prescribed dosage as instructed, friends and family search the alternative ethos but I had faith in my friends in the hospital, as they were still in my heart and eyes looking after me.

What a day…..

Geraldine fetched me from the land in reflection said it would be better if I went home instead of coming back later to feed and bed down the horses, in fact she insisted.

Once home I chilled and reflected on the days events, I'd managed the day well and had done some exercise too, ok, only walked a few hundred meters but I'd done it.

I made food for us all when her ladyship came home and we ate a hearty, healthy vegetable curry….

Sleep came quick and easy after food and a nice soak in the bathtub..

Monday, already awake and waiting for my day to kick start, Stephen wanted to meet and I was off to the Doctors for my bloods to be done and forwarded to the hospital. He picked me up and set off on the three mile drive across the city, one of those times we were stopped every set of lights and crossings. It took us near half hour, better off walking, I would've. We're on time for the appointment with nurse and she dealt with me, bye, out the door.

Where to go now, mother wouldn't be up yet, she used the excuse, she was retired and had all her life, she would actually just lay there reading. Stephen was actually in the mood for a stroll and meet someone for coffee, croissants with a nice confiture, that meant a deli so we headed to café au lait, coffee pukka, croissants fresh and home made strawberry jam. Just what the doctor ordered...

A nice morning was had and I then got a lift out up to the horses. Plenty to get on with what with the party that weekend. Geraldine had arrived about half hour after me hoping to get a chance to ride Tiep Tiep.. I obliged as always, like I had a choice. She rode well and was chuffed with his temperament, treating me to a nice piece of fish on the way home, great day and home for good nosh, bed and more of the same over the week.

The brothers met, drank copious amounts of tea and coffee, talked of golf days and sailing, skiing and stuff. Over food we revelled in some banter, on the golf club courses we met some truly interesting and inspirational friends, on the odd occasion the golf could be good too, just being with them was the kick I needed at times. Always afterwards we'd end up in a curry house or the clubhouse for a beer. In all these times I just strolled the courses, taking a well earned rest when I'd had enough, no drink either, my regime was set and I was going to win this one, I had to for this vast team we had in support. Coming all this way around this cross country course, falling, with three to go, I knew where we needed to be. They knew it too.

Slam dunk the Saturday night was fast Approaching, the final countdown with food and feasts of the best, were finally on us. I prepped frantically as the addition of English wet weather had already brought the altered venue, only a fifty meter nudge but the oven and fire pits were lit up. We had an evening filled with rain but it looked wicked, salads and bread were on the table, I'd made up curries to suit all types, vegetarian spicy tomato, a Goan curry that smelt far better than tasted, loads of chicken legs and lamb spiced curry with vegetables, all well ahead I found the radio, bottles of iced water and we chilled on steps for next hour or so, Joe occasionally being joyously distracted by the cooking of the birdlegs. First arrivals were Paul and Wendy his wife, armed with salad and sweet dessert of melon chips with lime and chilly flakes, of course the odd couple of cheeky ciders and a glass of red were also in the bag. Craig and his family were next to flock in, they had more ciders and desserts, David and Helen with three bottles of beer and a wine, David sniffed the air, curry I presume? Helen nudged him, giggling and continued in her admiration of the building I had created, more people more drink and food, fabulous company too, Stephen had arrived in his black shirt and shorts, the food was scrumptious, going down a real treat with little naan breads and bits done in the pizza oven, Mum felt great telling everyone how she so proud to have giving the boys lessons in fine cuisine, how it had made them the boys they are today

All in all we had made a good show and I was beginning to obviously tire somewhat, I took to the leatherback chesterfield, sprawling like the emperor of Rome, taking in the chat and laughter filling the cabin, it had been a great way to say my thank you….

I woke up at home with the flat door ajar, I'd been put to bed love her, she was an angel….

Just awake after sleeping in after last nights little get together, ping! Ping! More messages flying in from people who came last night. Paul's message was hilarious.

From my sober brother Paul, "all he wanted was Carts number so he could have the other 3 legs, carcass of the Portland lamb, do you think he'd mind me asking? I'll go get it, it shouldn't be too difficult as its only got 3 legs ha ha!."
He'd also had played a round of golf, it still only being 12.30pm, James my cousin had said hello through Paul's tom toms.
Still in bed at 2.45pm, I was loving it.
Well Geraldine was at work at the farm shop, and I had appointments tomorrow in both the morning and afternoon with the consultants, I needed my rest. Sticking to it.

Monday bath time and I was off to have bloods taken at the local surgery, by the nurse.
No coffee as of yet haha!
Coffee and breakfast and we were on our way over to the BRI, arriving early was Steve's little thing, never late was our Steve, upstairs for 1.30pm walking in we were very quickly seen by one of the team of consultants, he shook our hands, expressed how well he thought I looked

and was happily going to go ahead and book dates for surgery, he explained the full detailed procedure, how long it would hopefully take and all the necessary things that we needed to be sure of. As always before very concise with precise detail and emphasis on my role in all this, just keep doing as you are doing and we will see you on the 5th August. He left, we stayed to meet the anaesthetist upstairs, and have further checks done, all my statistics were checked, checked and checked again. More bloods were taken. The some exercise to show my strength. Some of which was recorded, Stephen joked, "he'd love a copy for, who's been framed."

That was that and we were too on our way back to Bath

Relayed the details to all and even managed to call mum, her tone expressing the relief she felt. I had a great sense of relief once more we had a plan, even more we had plan with a date showing light at the end of the tunnel.

For the time being we shared laughter and love, good times and some horrific golfing moments, Geraldine rode the horses we even helped her friend transport her lovely mare to another yard. Keeping me busy was in everyone's hearts and I just tagged along for the ride. Along the way making new friends seeing old too I was so blessed with brightness it lit up everyone's way.

Weekly events were much of a muchness bloods still done twice a week at the surgery, trips to see mother, coffee shops and hairdressers taking over the city centre, I very often strolled the rivers and canals, parks and streets, of this Georgian city. Not a day did I not see anyone. In fact totally the opposite, only that morning had Stephen asked if I wanted to get up to his for lunch, when my phone pinged I'll come get you I'm just in Peasedown, be 30 minutes, ok?
I thought it was from him, "no it's David I'll come up there and drop you home later." He said.
Lunch was nice, a Mediterranean omelette glass of iced water and a good chat over it all, strolling amongst the large felled trees. Tasting the dampness in the air, as I filled my lungs, didn't get this in a coffee shop in town..

We were all quietly blessed in this kind of life, but like most people we chose the more complicated way.

On the days Geraldine were working I'd often be around the family eating, golfing or just being.

We'd use the time to reflect on the good things which help to form this great bond between us. Managing also to keep our private lives more separate, brothers with their mother out was quite a nice thing. It also got mother involved in what was happening to me.

Letter arrived at home for me to attend the hospital, date of procedure was here and next stage had been set Tuesday 6th August 7.15 am A606 pre op. I shared the facts as I'd always done, the bigger the team the bigger the boat..

When Geraldine finally got to the land we sat down and chatted it through. "so there goes babe everything in place once again." I said, cuddles and back to our chores, well me to fall asleep in the lodge and Geraldine to muck out the horses, feed and get home, for supper. I'd already let her nephew Craige know we'd be down for Thai curry supper, only realising as I turned right on the lane then left heading south on the A36. The journey would only be about half an hour and we could share concerns once more with one another, if we needed to that was, it would also give us all some quality time. You know we just took the journey and admired the views as the sun dipped slowly to find it's pyjamas. On arrival we were soon greeted by the two yappers, the ferocious duo Bella and Hooper, Joe now in his element jumped from the landi and was straight in amongst it, chasing about the garden, skipping over each other and just generally being these incredible energetic balls of fur. Totally bonkers all three.

After a few minutes of their greetings we entered the house and could smell the cuisine. All cuddles and hugs from the two boys then I flopped into the cozy chair, Marshea brought me a chilled lemon water and asking if I were hungry, "you are aren't you?"

"Famished my lovely, famished." Holding in my tummy, we sat there until everything was gone, Marshea had done a great job once more of replicating one of their great friends recipes...The conversation was so far from what you'd expect. They had history of cancer and had lived with it most their son's life, albeit this way they just carried on living, much the same as we're having too ourselves.

We left their house just before 10.00 pm, it could take up to nearly an hour to get home from Wincanton.

My Sunday is my day as Geraldine had her work, so I just took up my usual Sunday stance on things, which brother would fancy breakfast, where and when? In their court, in fact it was funny as Paul's plans were golf and I wouldn't have minded a stroll so later that day we met and I watched him hash a few holes before retiring myself to the nineteenth for refreshments, sat in the bar area as it was far too hot on the terrace, I caught sight of some familiar faces, a few of my old pals from both rugby and golf, we had a great chat, they left in the knowing that, yes, I was remarkably well, considering all we had been through.

I gazed at the golfers as they struggled in the heat up the hill, longing for that iced drink. Trundling trolleys and sweaty brows were met at the door by the air conditioned cold air of the clubhouse. Paul was soon back in and had had a turn around in his game, he'd actually played well, believed in himself, as I did and was having too.

Paul dropped me at the horses, a fleeting visit as he had a busy week ahead, so apparently did Stephen and David, they still managed to arrange golf for later on in the week. All of us though...

Geraldine was already well underway and we knew that the next few weeks were ours to do what we wanted with, in respect of this we still rallied on our everyday doings and our routine hardly changed that much, horses like children need attention, need feeding and washing but most of all they can't tell you when they hurt, they somehow get it across, I know, I've seen you look at me in that way before.

The three of us walked around Bathwick meadows and watched as the sun sat over the channel some 24 miles away, a little to the right was Bristol and the Clifton gorge. We sat in the middle section of Joe's field as he felt he could just chase his tail in the long flowery meadow grass. We debated what we should have food

wise, is it going to be a salad meal or something more hearty? Decision made a split decision salad with green bistro leaves and beetroot, tomatoes and spring onions with salmon steaks in a chilli pepper sauce. A cheeky merlot for her and a sparkly water for myself. Springing to our feet we headed towards the car to get the provisions. Within 20 minutes we were home and Joe was eating his tea already, his crazy actions were to follow, tossing himself on our bed and pulling at the duvet...
We ate, bathed and were all in bed just after 9.45pm.

Was time slowing or just me dragging myself along sloth like? The week was already underway and we had a date for the next procedure, this meant I was already looking ahead, in a positive way, the week could be planned accordingly but my want was to spent it by doing the things we enjoyed, up with the guys at the cabins, maybe breakfasts with my brothers on occasion but most of all for me I wanted it to be unchanged from our ideal shaped world, Geraldine and Joe were a big part of all of this...

Geraldine had arranged with her friend Belinda that we could help her with her gorgeous horse Inca, inca was being taken for a few weeks therapy at a spa for horses some 50 miles away, but firstly she needed to be picked up and taken there. We arranged for this adventure to be on Saturday morning. The final details I left to the ladies, as any decent man should.

Paul text arranging golf evening for one night, just nine holes and a curry KO 5.00pm
David and Stephen confirmed to play and I was scorer Roo had yet to partake in an event this year, his work at the church was his enjoyment and he loved just being Roo.
So it was the three lads and me scoring set for Wednesday or Thursday night.
I met Stephen for breakfast and we went to see if mum wanted to join in, David couldn't he was busy working and Paul was at yoga classes.
We had a few hours at the little coffee shop in town opposite the station, mum and I both liked it there. The ambience along with the coffee was good and it was always busy with business people and shoppers alike.

Mum asked me how was I feeling about the next stages, relieved it was finally happening and knowing that I was happy gave her the best of my situation and she drew strength in her eyes almost immediately.

Stephen and I walked back to his car and we said our cheerios until the big golf day later in the week.

Geraldine had been to Belinda's and was on her way to the yard, she had given her a couple of hours work on her other horses, just grooming and husbandry stuff really, muck like our guys were about to receive and she may even have a little sit on Tiep…..

My thoughts were unblemished, no hills to climb, just that true path ahead of me, unlike the guys on the golf course that night, balls flying in all directions, machetes and axes were poised as too were the animals in the trees, as each fairway took its toll. Then suddenly a flash of inspiration from David's tee, the sun must've got in his eyes as his ball sailed 200-220-240-270 yards, straight and true, where did that come from? His nostrils flared, chest grew and he was the man, "I'm the man."as he stepped down from the tee, to a high five from me. The one shot that highlighted the evening, gave us the conversation in the curry house as we tucked into our supper like men who'd not eaten anything for months, complete banter filled the air. Parting ways in the car park we headed back across town to our loved ones at home.

Seemed like only yesterday that we had all been eagerly awaiting the test result concerning the extent of the liver damage and surrounding mass and now we're only moments away from the operation itself.

Saturday, up big breakfast of fresh coffee and cereals, orange juice and more coffee, out to walk Joe in the park, out to the horses and feed, turn out and and off to pick up Inca for Belinda. It could be a long day but it is Sunday, traffic shouldn't be too bad and I'll get it done. Geraldine and Joe were good company on the way down to Belinda's farm, we arrived dead on time, problems problems, A303 blocked and fires, we have to detour 40 miles, just to pick her up and it's even more coming back.

All in a days transporting, we got back to our horses later that day and took a late lunch at the cabin, a nice salad niscoise with extra tuna. Geraldine had to work Sunday so I insisted she rode this evening, and she did. Very well too. Home finally for 8.30pm. Hot bath and nice listen to music for a few hours...

Sunday, I got myself up to the park and sat in the sun, watched as the world passed me by, I lived in such a beautiful city with streets lined with majestic buildings of stone and tree lined parks, squares and rolling hills.

My love was at work carrying on in her routine, I knew I'd spend best part of the day in deep thought about tomorrow, David and Paul had decided to take me over to the hospital, they'd pick me up about 6.15am.

I called over to see David at his as it was 200 yards on from the park, his house always was so welcoming with the fresh coffee aroma and his culinary delights filling the kitchen, Noggin the ginger cat was stretched out on the long leather sofa, he always checked as I entered to see if

Joe was with me, no it's ok Noggin, he's not here, he stretched out in reply and rolled int the sun a little more. David and I had a fresh brew and chatted over the facts for tomorrow, pick up time etc and how we both were feeling, "how was Geraldine?" He asked.
My reply was as Geraldine had told me many times over the past few months,
" it's ok darling, it's ok."
I left there and headed back into town picking up some food for later along the way.

I had small things, preparation to do and knew I could do it easier if I were alone, music went on when I got into the flat, I packed my brown hold-all flip flops baggy clothes and wash bag etc. I was nil by mouth NBM from midnight so prepared a meal for my love and I.
I had medication to take too along with drinks at midnight then two preop drinks before 6.00am
The guys got home around 7.30pm and I had already run the bath for Geraldine, she'd done the horses too in addition to her work, a long 14 hour day, totally pooped, I made a nice salad with grains and rice, peppered mackerel,

washed down with a nice glass of wine, in fact her ladyship always had a glass in the bath... The night flashed before us and I awoke before the alarm, ran a nice bath, made some coffees and drank my two preop drinks, Joe jumped into my place on the bed as I continued to get ready, phone bleeped and Paul was outside, I leant across the bed and kissed Geraldine, she was still dozing and it made it a little easier to say goodbye, saying bye to Joe too I left the flat to the click of the lock and a sweet " I love you," in the distance, quietly I left the building, across the pavement and into Paul's car, we picked David up at his and drove directly to the main entrance, Paul dropped me and David at the door and we strolled into the building together, as we walked we were met by two familiar faces that had attended to me over the past few months, they showed us the way to the preop area and wished me luck, a hug of luck from each and see you later, up the ramp into the waiting area and we were escorted to one of the small cubicles for a quick going over of the days proceedings, including the necessary form signings and meeting of the team involved, the consultant greeted me with a firm handshake and smile as he went over the plan and actual procedure in detail once again, I signed the agreement and he said I'll see you later, the anaesthetist then entered and talked me through the steps before entering theatre, everyone happy and he left to join his colleagues in the theatre, my brothers and I sat there for about twenty minutes before I put on the gowns and was escorted to the theatre on foot, brothers and I parted with emotional moments as I was taken away, "see you all later."

In the theatre area I was placed on the bed and we chatted for a few minutes before I started that infamous back count from 10….

Waking up in recovery I could hear voices and I was totally aware of where I was, I recognised one of staff as she did me, my throats was dry and I could sense in my way I had not had as much work done as first thought, I asked the theatre nurse and anaesthetist how it had gone, no one was able to give me an answer, they were awaiting the surgeon to come see me, he was busy and would be hear as soon as. I felt under my gown and noticed I had small

incisions here and there, not too much. I called the nurse again and this time the surgeon appeared and asked how I was feeling, I asked him, what have you done, to which he replied, I stopped the procedure as I found some legions elsewhere and took advice from three colleagues who came in to the theatre and advise he stop as it could be very dangerous if these other markings are cancer, in fact the words he used was this was an inoperable situation. That's why we stopped I'm sorry Simon, so sorry, I took his hand and again found strength in me to say the words once more, it's not your fight my friend, we can do this, he left and I looked at the nurse and anaesthetist and said to them,
" people will always remember the way you make them feel, treat others as friends always. We shook hands and I drifted back to sleep...

When I awoke I was on ward A800 bed 17 three brothers and Geraldine waiting upon me, they asked what I knew and I told the best I could, David had received the call from the surgeon and explained what he knew, I explained too, we just needed it again from the surgeon but for now we knew even though it had not been successful it was still a success, so we have more to contend with and if need be a bigger fight….

We shared a few good hours of laughter and tears with mixed emotions of love and anger, however we still stood tall.

I ate a lot of crap that night and drank juice too, the staff were once again amazing towards me and left me to my own devices, after the guys had all gone I tried to settle through reading but to no avail, I was not getting any joy with sleep and reading so I played music and spoke with Geraldine….

All that pounded in my head was the heartbeat I felt as I lay in my bed with all these people, compassionate and so caring in their work, still looking after me, still wanting the best for me and my family, I felt I had let them down a little, many moments raced in and out of my head, the ball was in our court, where at the moment? I was not totally blindfolded and thought about that, I'm my work I would sometimes come up against the issues thrown in at the last minute, on many occasion I've felt that plan needs changing to be able to achieve the goal set out. Maybe this was one of those times where even tough situations that seem impossible, just need more time, a different thought, even a different approach. In my life I'd been here and did I know it, this was all I needed to help us all get through. A little light goes a long way, as I felt my body start to relax.

Andrew arrived very early the next morning, getting the bus over at about 6.15am, he came in pulled up a chair and we chatted, he knew I hadn't slept, so we amused ourselves through the day with light but heartfelt conversation. I took breakfast and sat there as Roo went to get himself a coffee, he had come over both in support but he wanted to capture the moment again and hear the surgeons words once more. The staff were as always very nice to me but I'm sure they felt my softness, avoiding this was the thing that gave them their angelic prowess. Roo returned with coffee and munchies, breakfast was finished and we walked a few laps around the ward, acknowledging the hellos and seeing the care in people's eyes made me walk taller than ever. I was absorbing the strength once more, making people talk...

After 4 laps we walked back in and I phoned Geraldine, text my family and brothers telling them I had yet seen the surgeon but as soon as I had news they would have it too.

After lunch the team arrived to see me, entering the room with his team the surgeon and I stood face to face shook hands and with few words acknowledged the obvious, we needed to talk, Roo asked if it would be possible to record the conversation, to which the surgeon replied, no problem at all, we went through the procedure in detail and he very kindly drew a detailed picture showing the scenario that made it even more clear. He repeated the whole thing and asked if I totally understood that if we had a chance of hope it would be determined by the results of the MRI scan that would be done imminently, those words echoed in my head " chance of hope" had things changed as last night things were inoperable?
I asked the question, to which I got the reply that changed my whole outlook,
"Simon if the scan results are in our favour and the primary tumour hasn't spread too far up into the hepatic ducts there is a possibility that

it becomes technically challenging, very technically challenging, all is depending on the scan results ok?"

My eyes filled as too did Roo's, I stood grabbed the mans arm and said the words again

" please don't let this be your fight it's mine and with you and your teams help here we will win this."

I shook and hugged him as brothers in arms would, his team and he turned and left the emotionally filled room, I turned to my brother, threw my arms around him and reiterated the words,

"Technically challenging, its possibly technically challenging."

Roo went into officious mode editing the taped conversation adding his word where necessary, all I knew is hat I had to tell Geraldine and my family the great news, and so I did.

So tomorrow a MRI scan, results in the MDT on Friday and decisions made again, in the meantime embrace the strength and enjoy the moment...

45 minute Scan in the morning and home for the afternoon, hugs all around the ward, tears

of joy and love, anxiety and pain but mainly friendship. Looks of concern and well wishes, a mixed bag full of emotion, we are not alone in all this, at times the emotions shown through others are so true, sincere that we can feel we've forgotten to say something, maybe a simple thank you.

My brother Paul met me and we once again headed back home to Bath, I made the usual calls on the way home, everyone delighted that again we were awaiting more test results, more chances. We called into David's on the way through, met with hugs and laughter. I sent Stephen a happy birthday message as he was away once again in Spain having Spanish lessons. I shared the discharge notes again with all so they were clearly in the know.
I also phoned Mum, the relief in her voice was so relevant. Although it had been a very hard one for all of us, my Mum was a rock, solid at times but with feelings of a mother's love, she felt it all, the pain and frustration and more, of course I was her third son…. A pain at times but still her son, her blood.

That night at home we just sat looking from the window admiring all we had and appreciating eachother's strength too. No words needed to be exchanged, the emotion filled the air, I took a bath and relaxed into a deep sleep for the first time that week.....
As I think Geraldine did too....

Friday and we let nothing change, Geraldine was up with the birds, out to the guys then off to work. I stayed in and caught up on somethings that seemed less important than ever now. It didn't last long before the urge to get up and go was in me, I took a lovely long walk in the park and people watched for an hour, my phone was busy with well wishes and the like coming from all over, lovely thing this Internet, unlike me to say it but in times like this it did a great job....

Wandering the streets of Bath with my mind so vividly clear of all things about me, brought a realisation, a trueness about me, why is it in times of trouble we differ so much?
Why do we live in fear, instead of living with it?
It's much more important to have felt the fear

and dealt with it than run from it, hide even, it's not facing our demons, it's actually quite good to grasp onto them and ride with them. We can do this we know for as a child, we come into this world and have no knowledge or perception of fear, it gets brought into our lives by others, through pain or persecution, or even psychologically. Yes, we need pain, hurt, to heal, to understand our bodies, mostly though to get through fear, the mind is the one thing we need to cleanse and continually empty….

I met up with David and Mum after they'd been to see Dad this morning, we ate in the café 250 yards from my place, I wasn't really that hungry but the soup looked good, thick lentil and sausage with crusty bread, glass of iced water and a flat white, appetite was good then? Mum and David had coffee and we had a good chat about Dad and his situation, Mum for once showed concern that I had not seen much of her over the past few months, she opened up and felt the pressure relief button slowly de-press.
A nice afternoon was shared there, totally unplanned but needed.

The remainder of the day was just spent chilling at home reading and listening to music from yesteryear, the jam, clash, old punk music and loads of Paul Weller, I woke to the door opening and Joe scampering across the floor towards me, he had a toy in his mouth and seemed to be so happy to see me, behind him was Geraldine carrying the shopping.

"How are you darling?" She then greeted me with a kiss.

"I'm good had a nice day doing, you know me?"

"How are you babe? How was work today?" The usual bombardment of questions before she'd even managed to get the shopping to the table. Joe's excitement lasted until he knew one of us was in the kitchen then he poised in his spot awaiting patiently his tea. Right under my feet, with big brown eyes staring up at me, following my every move, he was indeed a creature of habit, some bad, some good but loved all the same, once his tea was gone so was he, throwing himself around the flat, up onto every chair and bed along the way, finally settling on our bed with one of his toys. I ran the bath for Geraldine, pouring her a glass of red wine and a bowlful of nuts to munch whilst in the warm bath.

Saturday came and I had Joe for the day as Geraldine needed to work, we walked through Victoria Park and the Royal Crescent, on again to David's, West Ham were playing, early kick off too, the game was a real corker and even though the score showed a bit of a thrashing we had actually played well, they were just that much better.
David, Joe and I walked back through the park together as we had to get home also David had arranged to meet Helen after work, they would then steadily walk home, maybe stopping for a coffee or glass of wine on the way…
It was the height of summer and the streets were filled with revellers quite early tonight. We sat in the seat in the open bay of the kitchen window until the sun went down….

Sunday I completely missed as I fell in and out of sleep all day, the weeks events and sleeplessness finally catching up on me, I dozed throughout the whole day and when Geraldine came home from work I was in bed still asleep, she left me there, reminding that the best repair-time for the body is during sleep, I didn't argue just fell back off..

Monday I was woken by the birds on the window ledge, cooing in the morning sun, Geraldine already up, out with Joe in the park, Stephen wanting to meet for coffee a bit later and maybe up to his for lunch, plans change as we met in the Italian deli, I got things to sort this afternoon Simon sorry to mess you about, no problem always another day, no news from the hospital as yet about the scan was the most frequently asked question of the next few days, we all wanted to know, and when I say all I mean all, brothers, cousins, Mum, friends and old acquaintances alike, everyone needed an answer, I told them all I'd let them know as soon as I knew...
However I was as eager as they all were and decided that if we'd not heard by Thursday I would call the hospital myself.
After more meets with coffee and chats about life in general Thursday was upon us and I needed to call, I dialled, the answerphone

kicked in, I left the message. Job done, what should I do now?

Phone rang and it was an unknown number, I answered,

"Is this Simon it's the BRI in Bristol?" Came the callers voice.

"Yes it's me."

"Can you give me your date of birth and first line of your address."

"The conversation then sped up a little as the previous MDT hadn't determined the next steps and I was to be reviewed again this Friday in the next MDT, I know it's not the answers you're expecting but you are on our list. Ok Simon?"

We had news, ok maybe only holding off news but it was news after all, I relayed it to everyone and called my Mum too, she was delighted that at least we had something in the way of a positive.

I knew I would have messages in return asking more than we knew, it was human nature to query the question and answer alike, people just needed to know, in fact how it had become in all of this was quite surreal really, if they didn't know they surmised, made up, or even

elaborated upon, they were the first to fall foul of their own thought process. I kept the picture clear as crystal and told everyone the truth about what was happening in my world...
Have you heard? Or, did you know? wasn't true. People were funny about things they weren't sure about, given assumptions was an art especially us Brits were good at...

The weekend soon came upon us, funny as in hospital, time especially at times dragged leaving you slightly disorientated in the concept of time itself, no reason whatsoever gave us the true value of each passing moment, I now valued every second however it made me feel.

The three brothers met in Boston tea Party for a bite to discuss the plans for the following weeks and just have a catch, shame Roo couldn't attend, he had his reasons, I'm sure to see him soon anyway.
Stephen was on good form, as too were the others, I had to get down to the citizen advice bureau today to hand over some forms for Macmillan Cancer, the lady at the desk took them from me and I decided to walk back home

through the park, Geraldine picked me a few hours later and we attended our animals, well she worked I held the clipboard, she had off to an art now, making light of doing six stables, well she surely did. All done in less than an hour, back home and bathed in less than two, a true Wonder Woman.

Managing the next few days were funny as so much was in our heads, our focus had to remain strong and forward thinking. In all this we had held it together incredibly well, especially as we had been together through thick and thin, we never stumbled, showed the white flag even tripped, we were back to back in all we did.
A true testament of our love.
So proud and humbled...

"Roo, would like to meet up for a chat at some point love." I said.
"Go for it, whatever."
"He's in the park now I'll meet him and have a stroll, you want anything?"
"No it's ok, catch you later." She replied.

I slammed the front door and headed up towards the park, he was enjoying the twilight, feeling the need to share it, he called me. Words were few from Roo but I spoke enough for us both as we walked the dim lit streets of the city. It seemed to get chillier as we walked and felt the need to let him know, so we headed back to mine where we bid farewell. Bleep. Bleep.. I enjoyed that, from Roo. Enough said I fell into bed and gave my babes a kiss each goodnight.

Friday fell from nowhere and Paul had already made it into town with cousin James, we met in the café, 3 hearty veggie breakfasts, extra jam with toast with orange juice and a flat white later and we were set for the day, we walked to the car park in town, as entering the barrier lifted to the underground level my phone rang, it was the admissions at the hospital.
"Mr Simon Manister please." came the voice
"Speaking," I said
"This is the BRI Bristol you'll be getting a call in the next few moments regarding your procedure."

"It's going to be next Tuesday or Wednesday 20th-21st August ok?"

"Ok so I'll be getting a call soon?" I said.

"Yes, soon that's right, ok?" They hung up.

I looked at my cousin and brother, bemused. What do we do?

Wait for the call? Or get on with things? Driving around the car park was quite tense as we had no signal underground and Paul didn't want to miss this call, understandably so.

James and Paul had a conference call in about half hour at Paul's, so I tagged along with them. Phone poised to answer.

The next hour was indeed frantic, I had calls coming in, rejecting each, followed by messages of why did you reject me?

Then it came a direct call to me from one of the team,

"Simon, hello I have good news and I mean good news, we are to go ahead next week on Tuesday at 7.15am here at the BRI, can you make it? I will get you a confirmation call later today but your results were in our favour and we can operate next week, I know it's Friday and I wanted to be the one who told you personally. I'm so happy for you Simon."

"Oh! My, yes I'm ready I'll be there 7.15am Tuesday 20th August in preop, thank you so much thank you and your fantastic team." I replied.

We had a date, all was as originally planned just a little more technically challenging.

Paul and I left James at his and drove directly to Geraldine's work to tell her the news.

I walked in the shop past the counters and asked if I could see Geraldine in private, her boss was so thrilled by my expression she ran on to the shop floor and dragged Geraldine into the office,

"We have a date babe next Tuesday,no other spread and no other tumours so we just have the primary tumour to deal with, nothing else, that's it babe we have a date."

We cried, hugged and cried some more, thank you oh! So thank you, we looked at one another and I swear I felt so strong at that moment.

We'd made it through the storm and the lights were brightening on the horizon.....

Paul was patiently waiting in the car park and had obviously been sending messages out already, I joined in to tell everyone the fabulous news....

I had a confirmation call at about 4.00pm, I had also to attend preop the day before at 11.30am just to check my bloods and vitals, also to pick up my protein & preop drinks... maybe even see the anaesthetist. I had a date that was my biggest joy, we had made it so far and now it was in sight.

My brothers wanted to celebrate, maybe a curry of sorts, I called Geraldine to see if she minded, her words were inspirational, this is the least you deserve honey....

I arranged to go to the one in Box, well it was good and cheap and the boys could take their own booze.

Texting them the table booked for 8.15pm. We were in.

James came instead of Roo as he had to work in the church again.

We met and really had some fun, loads of giggling and laughter, reminiscing of days on holidays and weekend drives in the countryside with our folks, their strange friends and whichever waif and stray my Father had adopted that week. We left the restaurant fully charged and ready to hit the hay. I dropped David home with a hug and great smile before

returning home to my beautiful partner and
Joe.
 A great sense of being close to brothers made it
easier to sleep that night and did I sleep...

Alistair and Geraldine had arranged to ride in
the morning so she kindly left me at home, well
I did have a bit of a week ahead. I went fro the
flat to the park where I met our lovely friend
Lindzi walking her gorgeous little man Noah, we
strolled for about two hours generally putting
the world to rights, well I spoke Lindzi just
listened, no choice, she did it well, I didn't have
to nudge her too many times, just what was
needed a nice meander through the old park
and bend of someone's ear, I was in my
element. Not very gentlemanly I hear you say
but at least I walked her back to her car. She
made it very clear in the words she was able to
convey that I was certainly an inspiration and
should know this. Thanks again Lindzi a true
friend...
Upon getting home I felt the desire to take a
long bath and chill for an hour before the guys
returned from the stables. I did just that made
some green tea and drifted off in the bath,

hearing the noises of the shores that surrounded our infamous island, I drifted with the tide….

Mind at peace, true quietness released…

I had it all and more.

Saturday night we drove to Craige and Marshea's for a Chinese meal, lots of food later and with two regrettably bloated tummies we had an hours drive home. Mistake was made, it was a lovely evening but far too much fodder. I just wanted to get to bed. Wobbled in and fell on the bed, awoken by the dryness of my tongue attached to a sock on the bed. Yuk! Up various times in the night, some for water, the rest I'm unsure about, I was hanging and not a good example. I had to get up, do something, so I made a coffee and piece of fruit toast, Joe had already two second ruled my side of the bed and was watching me eagerly with one eye as I came back to the room tray of coffee and toast in hand, I've made coffee honey, you awake? A slight stir then rumble from under the covers as Geraldine rose with the words, "any water babe? A cold drink first please?"

I raced back to the kitchen ran the tap for a few seconds sliced a lemon and had two glassfuls myself before returning with her ladyships.
"That was a lovely evening but never again, that food, yuk!" She murmured, still half asleep.
" I know, I feel groggy as hell babe." I said.
"Still got me up this morning and you a coffee and toast in bed, hey?"
"Thanks."
I ran her bath for her as work beckoned again today, also the guys needed doing and we had to get more hay too from Nick over the valley, a long day again for us both, I also had to confirm with Roo the goings on for tomorrow and the preop situation, Stephen had already agreed with me about Tuesday, pick up time 6.00am at the flat. Roo on the other hand was always a little more vague and we would meet to discuss it today over coffee.

"I'm off then love." As Geraldine left with Joe, "I'll come get you about 5.00pm ok?" She said as she left.
"Bye then, see you later?" I replied.
With that I took to the bath myself, my eyes glazing over in the new morning sunshine, bells

were ringing across the city as people started to wake. Seagulls squawked loudly across the rooftops and songbirds sang in the trees opposite. A hot air balloon passed by the window with at least 8 people braving the flight over the valley. Deciding what to wear was my only issue of today, I'd already packed my holdall for hospital on Tuesday but hadn't decided on today's attire, tee shirt and sweat with combats and flips. That'll do nicely.

I had a nice green tea and listened to the early breakfast show, I loved the radio on Sundays, especially if I were alone that is.

I tried calling Roo and left a message, then again, this time he answered. We arranged to meet at lunchtime in Boston Tea Party, I got there early and had a bite to eat for lunch as I knew he'd most probably not want food. Was I wrong, he had a coffee and slice of cake then more cake with coffee, asking if I'd like one,

He got out his clipboard and then proceeded to ask the plan for tomorrow, consequently writing it all down even though I had a copy from the hospital in front of me. We chatted continuously for about two hours, which was nice, we talked over the situation I was in, how he felt about it all, but mostly just chatted. It was nice and relaxed.

Time was pressing on as I got up and said, "I'll see you tomorrow 10.00am outside yours ok?"

"Cool."

His reply.

Geraldine pulled up outside the flat and we zoomed over to get Joe before heading to the horses for evening feed and hay, we got there about 5.45pm and Geraldine fed as I hitched up the trailer to pick up the hay, as arranged earlier. Arriving at Nicks we were met by his wife and kids, the girls carried on and loaded twenty bales as I stood there helpless.

Nick and Bob his father arrived and asked about the next steps for me, in explaining all again it began to dawn on me that it was so close now, they wished us well and walked with us to the gate as we drove off the wishes continued.

Finally home and in need of a nice supper I knocked up a salmon and beetroot salad with mozzarella cheese, nice slices of brown bread and a pot of green tea and lemon.

Bed was calling and we crashed quite quickly, only stirring a couple of times, we slept through.

"Morning darling, coffee?" Came from the kitchen, as I heard the kettle click off.
"Ooh! Yes please babe, love one."
"What time you meeting Roo this morning?" She asked.
"10.00am outside his place, then straight over for 11.00am."
"I hope he shows on time for you?"
"He will." I said.
I got myself up pronto and took to the bathroom for a shave and nice warm bath, time was passing as I got ready and sorted everything I needed for the next few hours ahead.
I picked up Roo and we drove to Bristol, parking on the hill above the hospital, I remembered about having too much caffeine and drank water for the few hours before our appointment. We got there with time to spare and met the preop nurses who were attending me today, they took blood, observations and an ECG, weighed me and I was done, handing me my preop drinks she asked if I had any questions, out came clippy, just a few, to which

really the nurses answered as best they could but they were a little more than observation questions, more for the surgeons really, every one happy we were out of there. Tummy rumbling like a volcano now as we stretched our legs up the hill and drove back through Bristol in search of an eatery that suited the occasion.

I know in St George, Dad and I would go to this little café by the park and always have a nice nosh up, Roo loved it and ordered up a hearty lunch with mug of tea, me well I had poached eggs with tomatoes on toast and a tea.

"How long had you and Dad been coming here then?" Roo asked.

"About thirty five years I suppose, every time we came this side of Bristol we'd call in." I told him.

We shared a few stories about Dad and I, with work and stuff and headed back to Bath.

Along the A420, up over passed Tracy park golf club and onto Lansdown, before seeing the city below.

I dropped Roo off and drove straight to the horses and met Geraldine...

We finished earlier than usual and headed home for a quiet night before tomorrow's big day...

Stephen was on time and we were soon over in Bristol, he parked in his usual place and we walked up to the preop area together. It was only 7.00am and already becoming busy as we were escorted to our cubicle..
Introductions to the nurses and they took my details and observations once again, we filled in the necessary files and forms, leaving me to get into my gown and socks before seeing the surgeon and anaesthetists, who would go through the procedure once again.
This seemed to happen very quickly today and the surgeon whom I had met many times previously was as clear as ever as too was the anaesthetist, asking if we had any questions about the day, to which we both Stephen and I said no. Signing the consent forms and we were set, ready to go. The porter came to get me soon after, Stephen and I had a brotherly hug and moment as I walked to the theatre, the porter and I chuckled as we walked, we had met

previously on a few occasions and he always gave off an aura of confidence.

On entering the theatre I was greeted by the team and they talked me through the day ahead. The surgeon appeared for a moment and smiled with the team before they sent me off into my little place of tranquil skies, seas and mountains too, I was away....

"Hi Simon can you hear me?"
"Hi Simon."
"Hello again Simon are you ok?"

I was here and hearing things but obviously still very sedated, I could feel things about me and see people moving, my mind started to come back slowly as I heard more voices about me. The vagueness of the next few hours was so evident in that I could feel and hear but felt unable to speak, I may have been mistaken, it could have been me dreaming, the voices were so clear, then suddenly the voices became more recognisable in that they were talking with me, I heard them saying that everything was ok and successful, the surgery was long due to the fact that the main surgeon was pushed that little more by his colleagues who were in attendance, a real team effort and they had all been happy with the outcome.

Wow! I was aware of all this going on about me, the need to know more was important to us all, more so than ever before. I asked the nurse a few questions and drifted back to sleep once again.

"What time is it?" I asked as I woke,

"Morning of the Wednesday Simon, how do you feel?"

"You are in the intensive care, ok?" Said the nurse.

"Geraldine's here and we'd like to see if you can stand up please and sit in the chair." She said.

"Lovely, is she here now? Oh! please, can I speak with her?" I asked.

"Hi lovey, I told you we would make it didn't I?" Geraldine replied, "you certainly did darling, you certainly did that."

The physio and nurse proceeded to help me to my feet, I could see in Geraldine's eyes the anguish and anxiety of how it was going, almost unable to look at times, she grimaced my every movement, I sat back in the chair, exasperated and sweating from the moment...

We chatted with the nurses and had a bit of fun etc, I tried to drink some tea and have some cereal, only managing a few mouthfuls, I began to feel a little less anxiousness and pick up in my mood a little. Geraldine stayed a while and left as she saw me getting tired, I'd lost track of time and wanted to get up and move, I stood with the aid of the nurse and we marched on the spot for 60 paces, exhausted I took to the bed once again.

I think my brothers visited me, well I say they did but I may have been mistaken, I know that two of the nurses fro A800 came down to see me as they had heard I'd been in, then the physio was back again this time up 60 paces and rest...

Bloody hard work this being ill...

That night I had a fever and was in considerable pain as I felt cold, teeth chattering and shivers, painful throbbing in my stomach and chest area, the whole world seemed to be slowing down as I watched the frantic way these people had to work with us patients, they were incredible, reassuring and at times oblivious to others if they were concentrating on their own patient, the effects of the drugs I was on were sending me into a state of hysteria, I felt alone and scared, cold but was hot, hysterical when I saw my own reflection, all these tubes and wires about me, fans blowing cold air onto me, I was petrified, truthfully though I was in the best place, it was the drugs the painkillers were making me paranoid, I cried for Geraldine, my brothers and Mum and Dad, cried for help, for what seemed like eternity, then a doctor came to me, crouched before me and told me what was going on, I accused her of torturing me, trying to hurt me, and all she did was calmly reassured me, I was ok, in good hands and they were here for me, her quietness, calmness brought me safely back to where I needed to be, almost without saying too much her angelic serenity had taken my fear away and gave it back to me as strength once more.

I woke to the sound of people all around. I had slept a few hours and had thought about the events of the night, had I been dreaming? Was I ok?

No dream.

I was ok, but with a little fever, I had some water, a cup of tea and some weetabix, the nurse was off duty in a moment and came in to see me before she left for her well earned day off, she gave me a hug and wished both Geraldine and I all the best and was gone..

New day new nurse, as lovely as all the ladies and gentleman that had attended me, she gave me a bed wash and helped me brush my teeth, making me look handsome for the day ahead, the surgeon came to see me and told me the great news and how he felt about everything, I shook his hand and thanked him…. What a team…

Not long after my elder brother came in and spent a while chatting with me, he reiterated the surgeons words and we smiled at one another, a smile as big as the sky….

Things were going so well and we were now facing the recovery time, all my days had been to get this far and now I had to get back on track, strengthening both the body and mind along the way, I had the time to do it now and there was no rush ahead, we'd all made this possible, the team had used their knowledge and compassion as I had my strength and belief in both them and myself. The only way is up, how true is that.

Stephen left and to my amazement yet another
two friends from A800 came to see me and tell
me that I was to be moved there some point
today, already on the move how unbelievable is
that, I couldn't wait to tell everyone, I needed
my phone but had not used it for days so dint
know where it was, the nurse knew and fetched
it for me, a simple message relayed to
everyone, I'm on my way upstairs to ward A800
later today, ping!!! sent to all...
The tall young physio came to see me and asked
if I would like to get up, maybe try walking a few
paces?
"Come on then let's go,"I said.
"Okey! Dokey! Simon are you ready?" He asked,
Up and away, he took my elbow and we
proceeded to get up, I managed that ok, first
steps, turned around and I was off,
unsupported, just holding my drip-stand I
marched in the direction he said and strolled to
the next corner, "you ok?" he asked,
"feeling good."I said, "shall we go on?"
At the next corner we turned around and back
to me bed space, I was over the moon as I think
he was too, he commended my efforts and told

me he was happy with all. Happy days are here again, I was ecstatic...

I could've shouted from the rooftops, the smallest of things were so important to my world now, my whole life is about how I want it to be, simple as that.

Porter arrived and I was off upstairs, A800 room 27 lovely view across the trees, nice ensuite and a peacefulness on the corner of the ward, all my friends were here, so to was the air of caring and compassion, one could taste it....

I know it was hospital but these people were true angels, they'd ridden every storm with me, embraced me and my family through the days of joy and sadness, keeping me going, keeping me strong and encouraging me every step o the way, I had walked the circle hundreds maybe even a thousand times, the circle of life with them aside me. Never a doubt in my mind, always a belief that we can do this guys...

I called Geraldine and text the guys about the move, everyone the same reaction, how so soon? What, why so soon? Wow! That's such great news. I'd made the headlines, someone, somewhere, who didn't know me from the next person was being told, he's done it, he's moved upstairs already.

Humbled once more. What else could I say?

In all the comings and goings of the week just gone I'd obviously lost a few days but I'm sure that's the norm, I didn't know, would I be right in saying that it was Friday pm? I had to find out so asked the nurse,

"What day is it today please?" I asked.

"Hello Simon, it's Friday yes, welcome back to you, you feeling ok?"

A familiar face again, I couldn't believe it, however we look at people in life it's the first impression that will stick with them, these times gone by recently had left a massive impression on all.

I was beginning to feel slightly hot and an uncomfortable feeling started to take over my abdomen, had I done too much, strained, or even something like trapped wind again. I wasn't sure and this time I needed to ring the bell, my heart was racing and I was getting hotter, then the nurse arrived took my temperature, it was high, in fact a lot higher that they liked, they called for the doctor, who attended me straight away, I was in excruciating pain and almost doubled over in agony, more pain killers and more again. I wasn't feeling sick, just very hot and cramped in my chest and stomach, I slowly settled and calmed to rest a little, it wasn't a very nice time for me and being the weekend I just knew these people were busy. I almost felt I was in the way. My consultant had asked that I had a scan asap, he wanted to know as much as I did, the fact I hadn't eaten helped in the process as I needed to be NBM for a few hours beforehand and as I felt pretty constipated I'd not eaten anyway, I was coughing up glue like globules from my lungs and thus was irritating myself across my chest, the sweat was running over my chest and making my dressing soggy, hence they decided to change this, and in so noting my wound was seeping slightly on the outer edges they decided to remove a few of the metal staples, redress and make me as comfortable as possible. Feeling the urge to get up and walk, I did firstly a few paces then a few more, coughing clearing my throat and I breathed more easily, but it hurt in my diaphragm and below, a never ending cycle of pain, I went back to my room sipped water and tried to breathe deeply...

The porter arrived and I was on route, Sunday lunchtime and a scan, I was in and out in no time, doctor returned and I was prescribed intravenous antibiotics, starting immediately, I had an infection, not nice, but manageable, as for my tummy maybe again as I hadn't used the toilet for over a week, then maybe just maybe I was in need of a stronger laxative..

More drugs prescribed and hopefully we would be back on track soon.

I let everyone know and told my Mum too as I knew she was expecting to visit me soon, hang fire on that Mum I said and told my brothers the same, fact is I was ill and needed to rest and exercise when I needed or felt I could, whether it be early, late or whenever. I could hear in her voice she was disappointed and a little bit scared but I had to be the way I was for me and only me..

Everyone knew I loved to have visitors but I was susceptible to colds and infection, especially now. The slightest setback could be damaging to say the least, I knew how close we were and was not going to rock the boat now. This ship was sailing on a millpond, light breeze with no clouds on the horizon either, course set and sails up, we were so close.

Sleep well everyone as the day drew to a close. I sent everyone a rosy cheeked picture of me ready for bed….

Goodnight call to my beloved and away to me bed.

I saw every hour from 1am until getting up at 5am. A nice hot cup of tea and a blood taking moment, yes, I am awake thank you.

Observations done temperature still up but all else seemed ok, my pain was still there too about 3-4 out of ten so not too bad, but that was with painkillers so it could be more realistically 8-9. Just needed the antibiotics to kick in and take it from there, I certainly wasn't going to try that hard painkiller again, tramadol was not nice to me.

I tried pacing the wards more, even the staircase took a beating from time to time but I was hurting even more, I saw the nurse and asked if possible to have suppositories, she needed to speak with the doctor, perhaps a couple of hot cups of water would hit the spot, I tried the first three laps then the next cup,

three more laps and two flights of stairs,
imagining how now being too far away from the
toilet, what would I do?
In fear of messing up I started to rumble inside,
my stomach was like Vesuvius, only another few
meters to go, to go…..
Overwhelmingly happy, without pain, I took to
the shower, new razor, teeth brushed and pain
free I felt almost brand new. Like Tigger, I had
bounce again.

Observations done again and temperature still a
little high but coming down, I had to just keep
drinking the water and eating again. More
medication and antibiotics, I was sure going to
rattle before long. I pressed the nurse for more
laxative, better keep it going, than suffering like
that again. Now I could concentrate on the
mending side of all this, more positivity and
strength building needed, diet needed a boost
of proteins and goodness, nuts, fish and grains,
cereals and fluids were important too.
I made up a list for self improvement in all areas
and got on it straight away, nuts and grain were
downstairs in the shop, meats and fish I'd ask

Aaron or Geraldine, that's if I couldn't get it on the menu.

Mealtime arrived and I had chicken and pasta bake yoghurt and fresh fruit, the nurse with my meds also asked if I'd like a protein drink, Wow! She'd read my mind and I was allowed them with every meal. Morning noon and night. How great was that?

The feelings inside me were concentrating my mind to healing, dealing with the inside first and making that strong, I know physically I could get up and strut about, I also realised my mental state sat in a good place however the bloods and observations at times fluctuated indicating that although I was achieving my desire, I still needed to improve on my inner self, nutrition and fluid intake was one thing but mostly now I needed to listen wholly to the general consensus of specialists, consultants and nutritionists, physios and nurses, they were the ones watching me within, they knew if I was doing the right thing on the inside, my body had to regenerate, the liver had to repair and get strong again, this would put a massive amount of pressure in other areas and on the other organs, my diet had to be right so did my rest, rehabilitation after such surgery was so important and the staff knowingly monitored my situation in all ways, I was sure now that we had turned the corner, the light was brightening daily, still no rush for me just getting it right.

Geraldine came in that afternoon and we walked a few laps together and she was amazed by my strength in doing so, the staff were fabulous with her and gave her the support that they knew would lift her. We had some coffee and biscuits together and sat and chatted, tiredness was so evident in both of us but we had each other and held onto our spirit through our admiration and love.

I had so much support afar as I knew she did, at times it felt too much, we still used it to keep our strength, flourishing in the way people flocked together to guide you through.

Her Mum had been a big help in having Joe when she visited that on the occasions I could I'd phone her for a catch up, just to let her know I was ok and appreciated her help, Geraldine knew this was important to all of us as Rita was 87 and had a few issues in her life but she felt she was helping which gave her a feeling of doing, so important so she thank us for being there for her too.

When Geraldine left and within twenty minutes young Aaron arrived, laden with little gifts, we had a giggle and he was pleased to be around, we walked a few more circuits and then sat and chatted for a few hours about his world and how he thought he wanted it to be moving forward, he wasn't totally committed to his lady friend and felt that maybe he needed to move on relationship wise, choices, choices, and yet still only 24, he had a good attitude toward life and just needed to find a more directive approach, I told him that time will pass and your decisions now will set the foundation for you later in life, so take time for you, let the foundation evolve into something solid that no one could ever take from you. Firm feet as in good foundation are like the mighty oak they can ride any storm because they have good roots. He loved the way we spoke like this and always left smiling and happier than when he turned up. Hug at the elevator and he was gone back to Bath...

Bedtime for me and a cup of tea and goodnight message for Geraldine and I tried to get off myself.. sleep was difficult as I was in thought mode, I had been since coming back in, I managed two hours here and an hour there but not my usual way of sleep, maybe overthinking, I tried it all, counting, reading, music and even self hypnosis but nothing, more walking maybe, no I was tired but just couldn't get off. I absorbed it and thought no more about it, if it was this way then so be it, rest when I need, eat when I need and sleep, will soon follow.

Bloods taken at 5.15am and observations done too, a nice cup of tea and I sat up reading as the antibiotics were administered for the first time today, I read a little and listened as the night staff handed over to the next shift, fresh water in jugs brought in, fresh towels for shower, a polite way for them to ask me to get out the way whilst they make the bed, taking a shower was like playing twister I had to try to avoid my dressing and cannula getting too wet plus bend and twist to reach the bits that needed cleaning. Shaving was the same, once done though, I felt good, really good!!! All spruced up and for me it felt great. Self worth an importance of life.

Breakfast was served and I was dressed ready for the day, medication all done, belly full I again took to the ward for my regime filled morning. After six fastish laps I was pondering the stairs once again, could I do 4 flights down the lift then to the shops, four in the lift up, then walk the rest, sure I can. I took some cash from my pocket and started out telling the nurse at the desk I'd be back in half an hour. Getting to the shops was easy, lots of people about too, I bought a multipack of salted crisps and headed back up the long corridor to the lift. Straight in then four floors up out and walking the rest was a doddle, as I re-emerged on the ward I was met by the physio, "morning Simon, up and about I see, nice to see in fact." He said. I tried and I don't know why, I tried to hide the crisps. He so noticed my shuffling hands, and I felt the redness come over me, I was embarrassed by my actions, in buying crisps I had gone red, like a guilty schoolboy...

Why I asked myself.....?

Why indeed. I scurried away and as I approached my room, I glanced back over my shoulder, guilty of something…

The consultants and team came to my room just after 11.00 am

"Good news for us Simon your levels are all getting better and the fever seems to be settling well, we should be able to review the antibiotics this week with the intention of an oral alternative, everything is going well, you seem to be on the mend quite remarkably quickly. How do you feel?"

"Quite good, fine actually, ok in myself, finding sleep difficult but that's understandable I'm sure. I've got some irritation around the end of the incision site but it seems to be settling." I said.

"May I take a look as the notes say you had complained of irritation yesterday evening."

I took to the bed and lifting my shirt he noticed the redness and messiness of the dressing. Making the statement that the antibiotics would help with the inflammation and we will need to remove more staples today and re-dress the area as needed, ok?

They were happy nonetheless and left with the nurse attending the instructions as and when soon after.

That was brilliant news again and I was relaying it again to all..

I may have said this many times but my feelings were the more knew the better we all could accept the goings on. I felt so much more at ease with my knowledge, not that I dwelled in the dynamics of it for too long, I just knew myself, the faith was strength….

Marking with a pen the area affected by the redness gave them an indication of how the antibiotics were working, the pain wasn't like a sharp pain more of a prickly heat sensation, like stinging nettles, that set off more when the bedding or clothing rubbed against it.

Later in the day Aaron phoned me and asked if I was in need of anything as he was coming to Bristol, over to his sisters for some work then he'd call in a bit later, if I were up to it? I let him know he'd always be welcome and I didn't ever expect anything from him, it was something I had told everyone, everything here was fine, we wanted for nothing, plenty of food always at hand and drinks were in abundance. No need for my visitors to bring anything just themselves...

As it was he never arrived that evening, not even a message, just a no show, not a problem as I was a little sleepy and felt the need for rest, my sleep pattern was a little erratic and I had not really slept well since the operation, maybe me or just the effects of the drugs and pain relief. Just needed to sleep, anytime I could, I should.

Night closed in, it was becoming evident the cold was not far away, Autumn was finally upon us.

As the days were shorter my thoughts were turning in my head, how were I to cope at home, I know I have people all about me here and at home no one is ever far away but how will it be at home. See today for instance I've had no visitors as everyone is busy, they all have lives that turn day to day revolving all the time, especially Geraldine and my brothers, constantly busying either with work or family affairs, where would I fit in? Imagine being left to fend for myself, I'd manage, of course I would but just for instance if something simple like I fall or an anxiety attack, for sure I'd be scared, alone for long periods anything could happen, I'd be ok, I'm strong able and have an inner being that could pull me through. Scared to me means, this is healthy, it's good it needs to be expressed. Better a vacant flat, than an unwanted tenant....

The mind was so powerful and after my final medication and antibiotics I got ready for bed, it was only 9.45pm and already quite dark outside, the night-staff were busy and one of the nurses asked if I'd like a hot drink, a nice hot drink, I replied
"Ooh! Yes please a strong tea would be lovely, thank you."
"My pleasure sleep well Simon goodnight." As she pulled the door to...

Before the morning even broke I was awake, my sleep pattern was a little wayward at present, the need to be doing was important to me. I had spent enough time here, pondering, generally asking myself over and over the crazy questions one would expect in times like this, why? How? And for what?

Stupid as we all know that cancer has no reason, no definite trigger, and holds no boundaries, it affects the old, young, fit, in fact it has no real type, anyone can fall foul to its existence. It's how we live with it that matters, those around us try to comprehend, think that they understand the situation but reality is we as a whole don't know, none of us can explain why, how, or what but all of us can live with it. It's the living that is hard, trying to find the positivity, continually striving to go forward, smiling in the face of it...

We can do this, we most certainly have too, life is only time fragmented with memories, make them all for you and all around you. Treasure time and all it brings in your path, you are your own destiny, the truth is in you....

Sunshine was beginning to make a show as the nurses started their daily observations, I wondered if I'd have any news today from the team, any news was always welcome as each day was a step forward, closer to home.

Breakfast trolley was not too far away as I stepped into the corridor for a few laps of the ward, passing through the sun trapped hallway and into the reception area, everyone busying. The warmth of the sun was already creeping around the eighth floor as the place came to life. Many simply stayed in their beds, opting for the , why me? Status, I know some had no choice they were bedridden but there were quite a few who could have made more of an effort however chose not too.

I tried, at times succeeding to get a little motivation into some veins but it was hard, especially with the younger patients, all laptops and phones, no incentive to do anything, the physios and nurses tried and tried, sometimes succeeding but mostly a shrug of the shoulders was the only exercise of the day.

I still did my four laps, settling back for a hearty breakfast before showering and having a nice hot shave to kick off the day. Shorts and tee shirt as I sat in the corner as the nurse came in to make up my bed, neatly folded sheets and pillows plumped up, it looked so lovely, a clean bed, almost but not that inviting.

It's almost September and I'm finding it all a bit
surreal at the moment, what with one thing and
another, I'm feeling good in myself, reasonably
upbeat and jolly however the long journey
onward is quite daunting to take in, hard to
digest, will I get the support that's needed?
Thinking of the confidence that surrounds me in
here and how it may affect me once home, who
can I turn to? Whenever, I find myself heading
for a low, will I have the strength to express it to
others?
How will they bare up?
Coping for me in here is easy as I just talk it
through with whomever I feel, anytime day or
night. The uncertainty at home will be the one
thing I'll have to cope with. Especially as at
times I will be alone, Geraldine will be working,
my brothers, friends have their own lives. I will
have more time to reflect on the situation,
taking in the facts with an air of resilience will
be my strategy, maybe I'll have more support
than I can cope with, too much at times and I'll
want to run and hide, maybe just maybe..
These things are healthy to live with, easily put
in their place but only when it deems to be
necessary, thinking to far ahead is like trying to

climb a mountain blindfolded, possible but very dangerous. Each step should be taken in caution of the next movement or thought. Take it as it comes, you'll get there in time.

The day seemed to be settling nicely when the consultant tapped the door, his news was music to my ears, all my issues were balancing out and if things were still improving after the weekend I could be home next week. Such great news and my smile showed the elation I'm sure, they left and I was straight on the media networks sharing my joy...

Lunch was a treat and during it I had some beautiful messages from all over, my little brother Roo was thinking of bringing Mum to see me if I was up for it. Of course I was, we had great news and I couldn't wait to share it with Mum...
People were amazing, putting my mind at ease over the support issues that arose earlier that morning.

Evening approached fast and I didn't have any idea if Roo and Mum were coming, I was beginning to think maybe not as it was knocking on a bit and I'd been up since before the dawn. Then there she was in all her glory, Mum had arrived with Roo in tow, she looked really well, made up in fact. She sat in the chair next to the bed and of course made an absolute fuss of me. It was already 7.30pm and Roo decided to let us have a bit of time alone, we spoke about things that mattered to her, especially the Dad scenario, he was in a good place but Mum at times was a little low, she needed company and found it hard to be on top form all the time, Dad had always been around Mum and obviously had overshadowed her, where was he now? Away from it but surrounded by the care of the home, much the same as me now, I could sympathise with Mum, especially now with what was happening with my life.

The fact we had a good chat about it, expressing concerns and being honest had eased her anxiety towards my situation a little, when Roo walked back in the mood was good and quite chilled, she seemed to tire quite quickly, as I did too. I walked to the elevator with them and they left in the knowing that all was good, I was coming home soon, very soon. Ping!!! the

elevator door opened and they were on their way, I walked a few laps before finding a film to watch on the small hospital TV....
Drifting in and out of sleep, every movement, ticking was registered in my head....

Sunday 1st September 2019. A new month, new day with new energy that filled the room to the brim.
I was in my element, full of it, the nurses doing their thing and my happy feet were in the mood to walk....
6 laps before breakfast, 2 teas later and all fresh from an invigorating shower. The worlds my oyster and I was the pearl....
News I never did.
Papers never read.
Tabloids ignored, I lived as I deemed suited me.
What would my ideas solve for others?
Mostly nothing as I wasn't important...
Still a gem of a guy though...
It had got to the stage now where I treasured every moment as we all should. My life this year has been incredible, riding my horses in January and February sunshine, continuing on the lodge, making furniture and changes as I went along

and skiing in March with our friends in the Alps, we'd done it all and had this battle going on too, yes I say a battle a true fight, but this was mine, my conflict, proving to myself all along that no matter how hard the struggle all one needs is belief and a good team behind you, and by the love of all, I had the team of teams. Truly inspirational and devoted to this cause.

My heart was true and myself humbled by their compassion, in truth I owed all, however they asked for nothing, just thanks and a smile...

The day was made even more special as when the consultants came to see me, they brought me the news that I may be home this coming week, a lot sooner than we had all expected. All my levels were good and I had made fantastic progress, in fact the surgery had been successful and I was still here, I was liberated and felt so happy with the way my life had brought me this new chapter, I captured the smiles as the consultants left the room. My news again shared with everyone, I knew I could be kind to myself now as I had overcome the fears with them, beaten this with them, also fulfilled our hopes for all of us...

Fear is in all of us, it's how we manage our emotions that make us the people we are, anger and fear are so close in the way we understand their meaning that we lose our way trying to get our point across. Don't get angry or scared just follow your heart, breathe and take in the moment and the fear will subside.

The Sunday afternoon passed, contented was I in the knowing that all was as well as it could be I listened to some good old reggae, proper good time relaxing music, old school reggae. It brought the day to an end and eased me into a deep sleep much before I had thought I would. Only when the nurse came to give me my medication did I realise I'd yet to have called Geraldine and it was after our bedtime goodnight, whoops!!!

"Sorry babe,"as I heard the voice answer.

"It's ok I'm not in bed yet, it's been a long day and we have just come in from Joe's walk before bed." She said.

The chat was lovely as we recognised how the day had lifted our spirits and made way for our new life ahead...

"Love you babe, goodnight." The last words of the day and sleep was imminent…

Monday came with the usual needles, prods and pokes, and that all before I was out of bed, the funny thing was I had a feeling today was going to be on point. I was going to have a great sense of being, as the sun rose I noticed the magpies in the trees over the road and how they ritually paraded themselves at this time of year. The world seemed to change too, trees lost there greenness as they took on the autumnal colours of yellow through to burnt amber, even the clouds moved more freely, faster and with more ferocity, things had more purpose, the window cleaner was working away on the ground with his pole extended to the 8th floor, he couldn't see the dirt caused by the birds but I could and indeed he must've felt someone was watching him as he spent minutes in the corners up and down, up and across with more assertion, but he got it. Staff arrived wearing jackets and coats for the first time in ages, as if September meant cold. Porters in long trousers, umbrellas in hand…

After a while the sun broke through and the heat transmitted through the windows, engulfing the corridors and staff decanted their Cardigans and sweaters, complaining of the heat and how the air-conditioning was not good enough... September a month of change...

I had breakfast and was reading when my phone bleeped, it was Geraldine on her way over and did I need anything, a clean shirt and shorts as I fancied a spruce up. She knew what I meant and obliged me.

On her arrival the lunch was being dished up so she went upstairs and got a coffee and snack out of politeness. We chilled and reflected over the past few months, mainly over our support for each other and how we came through this ordeal, somewhat we both were quite surprised how strong we both were, mentally and physically. We knew we had it in us as we'd had a few moments and tragedies already behind us. One thing for sure though was we stood tall when faced with adversity, we had a definitive resilience...

Once more the time flew between us and Geraldine's time on the parking meter was up.

Came, gone but the moments shared were important to us both.

David called asking if I had any news on homecoming as yet, he was about most of the week apart from tomorrow but as I'd not heard then maybe it wouldn't be that soon.

Set in my routine I did more meters around the ward and decided to maybe watch some Monday night football on the iPad.
I found some rugby league match and watched it for an hour before finally giving in to the fluffed up pillows, getting into bed was lovely as I curled up for the night, final meds done and a goodnight from my lovely and I was away, dreamland...

Tuesday so good for me,
Awake and slept well, I'd managed to fill a few urine bottles in the night and slept straight through after, incredible how something so trivial could mean so much, my input and output determined so much about me, food water and fluids were all a big part of the healing process, as too was sleep, solid sleep,

not napping or boredom sleep but trusty old fashioned shut eye. Rejuvenated was I that the new day brought a change to my breakfast desires, I really fancied toast with marmalade and lots of it, washed down with breakfast tea, hospital style. Crumbs in my dressing gown and an itch to my tummy I needed a good old clean up, teeth and shave first followed by a complete body wash, avoiding the battle scars and areas of tenderness. Perching on one leg with flannel in hand I managed to reach the areas quite easily. My core and tummy although very sore and severed across over eighty percent of my stomach amazingly didn't need to be engaged to balance me, I was chuffed with how I managed, drying myself and dressing were the next big moments of the day. Ok I had managed over the last week to put on the robes and dressing gowns but today I wanted to dress to impress. No one in particular just myself, I wanted to feel more like me. So I did exactly that I put on my shorts, a flowery shirt and my loyal lovely flip flops.. my old self I was and ready for the world to see..

Setting off passed the central nurses station my eyes were met by the physio, he stood to say hi and admire my style, he also commented on how impressive my walking was, to be honest I was commended by a few members of staff and patients alike, one guy even asked if on the next circuit he could join me for a lap or two. Obviously I didn't hesitate in having a walking partner, what's good for the goose and all that. I loved it, and people did too, the bright shirt and autumnal sunshine had brought a spring like freshness to the ward. Easy to do when life's that great, and that's how I felt.

After more walking and cheerily set smiles for everyone my eyes met, I walked back into my suite, the consultant who had performed the procedure was soon to follow me in, with a good morning, exchange of pleasantries, he began to tell me how pleased he was, also reiterating the fact that he had been egged on in the theatre by three colleagues, who insisted he went above and beyond, so heartfelt and honest it brought me to tears, my hands engaged his in a firm handshake that for me would never be enough, his smile and eyes lit up as I told him I wonderful this had all made me feel. We spoke of how the operation was and how much still needed to be done but the general consensus amongst the consultants and all involved was we were on the right track. Just time now, strength building time and plenty of recuperation too.

"Take your time Simon and I'm sure you'll be home soon, ok?" He said as he left the room... Floating on air I could feel the whole world carrying me as I took off to share my news, I told the nurses, cleaners, housekeepers and anyone in my path. I walked to the big window overlooking the city and told the world. Sitting in the sun drenched window my emotions were to strong and for the next minute or two I found myself crying, tears of joy, relief and sadness too, there are many people here who have no sense of how I felt and maybe wouldn't comprehend it but my days ahead were all for me now, as selfish as it seems I wanted to share each moment in the knowing that we have one chance so don't let it pass you by... share it with all, no matter who, just embrace life ....

I sent a video through social media of myself joking about how I was getting on the mend, after all this surgery I was finally getting on the mend..

Responses were quick and quite amusing, some asking if I were still on morphine, if I'd had too much, whether they were considering a frontal lobotomy next and even one asking if I needed psychiatric help after being in hospital for so long.

Nothing as queer as folk. Hey!!

My brother Stephen summed it up in one.

He's back on the tramadol….

As if….

About an hour passed by when the team entered with more great news, I tried to turn off the iPad as I was listening to some lovely music by Ennio Morricone, dropping it onto the bed I thumbled and eventually got control shoving it under the pillows as one of the consultants began to tell me the fabulous news, firstly he reiterated the words I had heard earlier, then he commended me for my part in all this, before the news that I was in such good shape they felt that I could go home that day, they all smiled in unison as he explained all about how they had had a meeting and agreed the way forward for me was to go home and get stronger, keeping up my good work and forward movements, they also would be having more meetings and I would be contacted very soon for a follow up appointment and consultancy to establish the next steps. Another consultant expressed her admiration and agreed that I would be better going forward at home, one by one all of the team in the room shook my hand, wished me well and said their goodbyes, the tissues were soon to follow.

How often could I say thank you in such a short time, I don't know but it would never have been enough, my eyes were full and heart too. Nurses came in and shared my joy, so too did the guys working on the ward, a young doctor I had befriended came to shake my hand and wish me well, sharing a moment of pure emotion as he returned to his tasks. No words needed as I approached the sister and her team in the central area, just hugs and well wishes, everywhere I turned I had jubilant eyes following me.

The next few hours were filled with all kinds of moments, questions and answers, medication needed sorting, staples and dressings removed and where necessary redressed, bag packed and lift home arranged, last goodbyes to a few members of staff, then came the moment, they needed my room, another patient needed a bed and I was on my way to the discharge lounge. The next few minutes were and will be with me forever as I crossed paths with all in the ward, the porter had to stop at every pair of feet on the ward as I was given hugs, handshakes and best wishes as my eyes glazed over once more, I left ward A800, the people I had shared the most incredible fight and somewhat surreal journey with, for now but not forever as I promised to come see them…

After all they were my family, my guiding light and my corner in all this…

I was going home…..

Printed by Amazon Italia Logistica S.r.l.
Torrazza Piemonte (TO), Italy

11057100R00153